THE CARMICHAEL LECTURES, 1921

LECTURES
ON
ANCIENT INDIAN NUMISMATICS

THE CARMICHAEL LECTURES, 1921

LECTURES ON ANCIENT INDIAN NUMISMATICS

D. R. BHANDARKAR

GYAN

Published by

GYAN

Gyan Publishing House
5, Ansari Road
Daryaganj, New Delhi-110002
Phone: 011-47034999, 9811692060
E-mail: books@gyanbooks.com

Distribution Network
gyanbooks.com
India, USA, Canada, UK, Australia, France

ISBN : 978-81-212-4562-3 (HB)
First Published, 1921

2nd Impression 2020

Printed at: Gyan Press, Delhi.

Lectures on Ancient Indian Numismatics
Author: D. R. Bhandarkar

DEDICATED

with

Profound Respect and affectionate Regard

to

My Father

Dr. Sir R. G. BHANDARKAR,

Master of constructive and suggestive Criticism

In all branches of Indology.

PREFACE

In 1918, thanks to the President of the Post-Graduate Council in Arts, a course in Ancient Indian History and Culture was introduced for the M.A. degree of the Calcutta University, and various lecturers were appointed to teach the various subjects falling under it. Thus a young promising scholar had been appointed to teach "Numismatics," which formed part of "Archæology," one of the Groups comprised in this course. He was placed under me for some time for being trained in the subject. He was working very hard, but just when he was fit and ready to lecture on "Numismatics," circumstances forced him to leave us. As there was none else in the University at that time who was sufficiently conversant with this subject, there was no recourse left but for me to teach it. I was therefore compelled to devote my special attention to it. I was not, however, sorry for it. For that convinced me, once again, that there was hardly any field connected with the Ancient Indian History and Culture, where research work was not possible. When I began to revise my knowledge of numismatics with the object of preparing myself to lecture to the classes, I thought that it was practically an exhausted field, containing hardly any scope for further work. Soon, however, I was undeceived, and found that even here much new and good work was possible. This work, of course, I had to do, when I was lecturing to the "Archæology" class. As some of my conclusions and points of view were thought by my friends to be interesting and worth placing before scholars, they were embodied in a course of five lectures which I delivered last cold season before the public in the University. It is these lectures that have been published in this volume, and I am glad they are now before scholars for their constructive and helpful criticism.

The Index of this volume has been kindly prepared by Mr. Jitendranath Banerjea, M.A., who is now lecturing on "Numismatics" to the "Archæology" Class of the University. In regard to the proof-reading and the great help I required in the preparation of these Lectures, I am indebted to Babu Nanigopal Majumdar, M.A., who was my pupil some time ago and is now one of my Assistants in the University.

D. R. B.

CONTENTS

			Page
Lecture	I.	Importance of the Study of Numismatics ...	1-36
,,	II.	Antiquity of Coinage in India	37-75
,,	III.	Kārshāpaṇa : its Nature and Antiquity ...	76-123
,,	IV.	Science of Coinage in Ancient India ...	124-166
,,	V.	History of Coinage in Ancient India ...	167-212
Index		... ...	213-229

LIST OF ABBREVIATIONS.

AA—Ariana Antiqua.

ACMC—Ancient Coins and Measures of Ceylon.

AI.........Ancient India.

ASI-AR—Archæological Survey of India Annual Report.

ASIR—Archæological Survey of India Reports.

BG—Bombay Gazetteer.

BMCGSKI—British Museum Catalogue of the Coins of the Greek and Scythic Kings of Bactria and India by Percy Gardner.

BS—Bibliothica Sanskritica.

CAI—Coins of Ancient India.

CCGD—Catalogue of the Coins of the Gupta Dynasties.

CCIM / CCIMC—Catalogue of the Coins in the Indian Museum, Calcutta, Vol. I.—by V. A. Smith.

CCPML—Catalogue of Coins in the Punjab Museum, Lahore, Vol. I by R. B. Whitehead.

CICBM-AKTB—Catalogue of Indian Coins in the British Museum of the Andhra dynasty, the Western Kṣatrapas, the Traikūṭaka and the Bodhi Dynasties.

CL—Carmichæl Lectures.

CMI—Coins of Mediæval India.

EI—Epigraphia Indica.

ERE—Encyclopedia of Religion and Ethics.

HASL—History of Ancient Sanskrit Literature.

IA—Indian Antiquary.

IC—Indian Coins by Rapson.

IG }
IGI }—Imperial Gazetteer of India.

INO-ACMC—The International Numismata Orientalia-Ancient Coins and Measures of Ceylon.

INO-CSI—International Numismata Orientalia-Coins of Southern India.

IS—Indische Studien.

JA—Journal Asiatique.

JASB—Journal of the Asiatic Society of Bengal.

——N.S.————New Series.

JBBRAS—Journal of the Bombay Branch of Royal Asiatic Society.

JBORS—Journal of the Bihar Orissa Research Society.

Jāt—Jātaka (Cowell's edition).

JHAS—Journal of the Hyderabad Asiatic Society.

JRAS—Journal of the Royal Asiatic Society.

MASI—Memoir-Archæological Survey of India.

Nchr—Numismatic Chronicle.

NO—Numismata Orientalia.

NO-AIW—Numismata Orientalia—Ancient Indian Weights.

SBE—Sacred Books of the East.

TSS—Trivandrum Sanskrit Series.

VP—Vinaya Piṭaka.

ZDMG—Zeitschrift der Deutschen Morgenländischen Gesellschaft.

LECTURE I

IMPORTANCE OF THE STUDY OF NUMISMATICS

Numismatics, as you are all aware, is a science which treats of coins. Before, however, we begin our study of this science, the question must arise: what is the importance of this study for the purpose of the ancient history of India. This question is natural, because it is generally believed that numismatics merely confirms history but seldom modifies or amplifies it. It must be noted, however, that this remark holds good in the case of the history of other countries only, but not of India. No connected written history of this country for any period prior to the Muhammadan conquest has come down to us. We therefore have to construct it as best as we can out of the materials at our disposal. These belong to two main classes, the first of which consists of contemporaneous works whether written as panegyrics by Hindu authors or as descriptive accounts by foreign travellers and historians. The second class of materials is of a more important nature, and comprises epigraphy and numismatics. In the construction of the ancient history of India, coins have therefore to be classed with inscriptions in point of importance. Numismatics is thus like epigraphy an important source of ancient Indian history; in other words, it helps us to construct history and does not merely corroborate it.

If numismatics is thus a source of history, as important as epigraphy itself, can it be shown, it may be asked, to shed light on the different aspects of the ancient Indian history? Let us take the Political History first. It is hardly necessary for me to dwell on this point, because many of you are already aware how much beholden Political History is to this science. In a book of the ancient history of India, how often we read about the Indo-Bactrian Greek, Indo-Scythian, Indo-Parthian and Kushana kings, whose might overshadowed the north of India from about 250 B.C. to about 300 A.D. and who were either ruling conterminously or supplanting each other in succession? What would have been our knowledge of the Indo-Bactrian Greek princes, if we had not had their coins to help us? Of course, some Greek historians like Justin and Strabo have preserved an account of some of them, but this account is of four or five princes only and ranges scarcely over half a century. On the other hand, a study of their coins reveals to us no less than thirty-seven such Greek princes,[1] whose sway extends over two centuries and a half. The condition of their contemporaneous barbarian potentates, *viz.*, the Indo-Scythians,[2] was even worse. Who would have heard at all of Vonones, Spalirises, Spalahores, Spalagadames, Azes I, Azilises and Azes II, if their coins had not been found? Certainly no historian or traveller, Indian or foreign, has preserved any reminiscences of them. Again, it is their coins which not only give us their names but also enable us to fix their order of succession.[3] The Indo-Parthians, who overthrew the Indo-Scythians, do not seem to have fared better. Of course, there is an epigraphic record of Gondophares, the founder of the Indo-Parthian dynasty, and there is also a reference to him, perhaps of a nebulous character, preserved in the Syriac version of the Legend of the Christian Apostle, Saint Thomas. But what about his successors, Abdgases, Orthagnes, Pakores and so forth? If coins of these latter had not been recovered, should we have ever known anything about them? It is true that in regard to the Kushanas we are luckily in possession of a

---

[1] *CCIM.*, 5-6.

[2] I agree with Mr. Whitehead in calling them Indo-Scythian. My reasons have been set forth in *IA.*, 1911, 13, n. 15.

[3] I was the first to fix this order of succession in *JBBRAS.*, XX, 284 & ff., which was accepted by the late Dr. V. A. Smith in *ZDMG.*, 1906, 59 & ff.

fairly large number of inscriptions of Kanishka, Huvishka and Vāsudeva. But what about their immediate predecessors, Kujula Kadphises and Wema Kadphises, who were the first to establish and propagate Kushana supremacy? Are we not indebted for our knowledge of these rulers to the study of their coinage? Perhaps the most important service done by numismatics to political history is in connection with the Western Kshatrapas who ruled over Kāṭhiāwāṛ and Māḷwā. The founder of this dynasty was Chashṭana, who has been identified with Tiastenes of Ozene (Ujjain), mentioned by Ptolemy, and has been assigned to circa 130 A.D. Here too, as in the case of the Indo-Bactrian Greek princes, many names of the Kshatrapa rulers have been revealed by their coins, which, again, as they give the name and title not only of the ruler but also of his father, and, what is most important, specify dates, enable us to arrange them in their order of succession and to determine sometimes even the exact year in which one Kshatrapa ruler was succeeded by another.[1] Nay, a careful study of their coins enables us even to find out where and on what three occasions there was a break in the direct line from Chashṭana.

Let us now turn to the Administrative History of India and see whether the study of coins has

---

[1] *ÇICBM-AKTB.*, Intro., cliii—clvii.

ever proved to be of any use there. I hope you have not forgotten the two lectures on Administrative History which I delivered here two years ago. I had then occasion to bring into requisition the various items of information supplied on this point by Indian numismatics. Especially in the second of these lectures, which was concerned with the Saṃgha form of government I drew your prominent attention to three types of Collegiate Sovereignty denoted by the terms Gaṇa, Naigama and Janapada. Gaṇa, I then told you, was an oligarchy and was thus a distinct political form of government. This conclusion was in the main based upon Chapter 107 of the Śāntiparvan of the Mahābhārata, but received corroboration from what we knew from numismatics. At least three types of coins have been brought to light which were issued by three different Gaṇas, *viz.*, the Mālavas, Yaudheyas and Vṛishṇis. [1] That all of them were Gaṇas was already known to us from inscriptions and Kauṭilya's Arthaśāstra. And it may, therefore, perhaps be argued that these coins teach us nothing new. Nevertheless, it must be acknowledged that they possess great corroborative value, which cannot be ignored in a subject connected with Administrative History, which is still in its infancy. Although in respect of Gaṇa numismatics does not

---

[1] *CL.*, 1918, 157 & 166.

thus furnish us with new information, its value in respect of the other forms of Saṃgha government cannot be denied. In that second lecture of mine on Administrative History, I have clearly shown that side by side with oligarchy, democracy of a two-fold kind was flourishing in ancient India, one styled Naigama which was confined to a town, and the other Janapada which extended over a province. Of course, I am not here referring to the power which the people of towns and provinces, called Paura and Jānapada respectively, sometimes wielded in the administration of a country, and which is often alluded to in the epics and sometimes in works on law, but which was never of a political character. I am here referring to those cities and countries which enjoyed political autonomy and whose existence has been attested by coins alone. I hope you remember I mentioned one type of coins found in the Punjab on the obverse of which you find the word *Negamā*, *i.e.*, *Naigamāḥ*, and on the reverse such names as Dojaka, Tālimata, Atakatakā and so forth, and told you that they were really the civic coins struck by the peoples of these cities.[1] This, no doubt, reminds us of similar coinages of Phocæa, Cyzicus and other Greek cities,[2] and further points to the fact that the Naigama or civic

[1] *CL.*, 1918, 176.

[2] *The Gold Coinage of Asia before Alexander the Great* by Percy Gardner, 32.

autonomy was as conspicuous among the Hindus of the old Punjab as among the Greeks on the Western coast of Asia Minor. That a country autonomy, or Janapada as it was called, was not unknown to India is similarly clear from a study of coins only. Thus we have two types of coins, one of which was issued by the Rājanya Janapada and the other by the Śibi Janapada of the Mādhyamikā country.[1] A few other interesting facts connected with Administrative History are also revealed by numismatics, but it will take me long to mention them. Two administrative puzzles furnished by it I will, however, mention here by way of curiosity. Those of you who have critically examined the coins of the Indo-Scythian dynasty must have already been faced with one of these puzzles. Four kings of this family are Spalirises, Azes I, Azilises and Azes II. Now, the peculiarity of the coins of these princes is that over and above those each issues in his name alone, he strikes coins conjointly with his predecessor and his successor, but with this difference that in the first case his name appears on the Kharoshṭhī reverse and that of his predecessor on the Greek obverse, and in the second case his name on the Greek obverse and that of his successor on the Kharoshṭhī reverse. What is, however, puzzling is that the

[1] *CL.*, 173.

titles of the prince on the Greek obverse are of exactly the same political rank as those of the prince on the Kharoshṭhī reverse. Thus to take one instance, *viz.*, that of Azes I and Azilises, the former is styled *Basileōs Basileōn Megalou Azou* and the latter *Maharajasa rajarajasa mahatasa Ayilisasa.* Here the titles *Maharaja rajaraja mahata*, which have been coupled with the name of Ayilisa, *i. e.*, Azilises, are the exact translation in Prākṛit of the Greek titles *Basileōs Basileōn Megalou* associated with the name of Azes. The titles are thus exactly identical, showing apparently that the two rulers wielded the same degree of political power. But how is this possible? because Azilises is the heir-apparent and Azes the real king. According to Hindu polity a Yuvarāja cannot possibly be assigned to the same political rank as his father the Mahārāja. Such was also not the case with the many foreign tribes who established a kingdom in India. Take, *e. g.*, the Kshatrapa dynasty which held sway over Kāṭhiāwāṛ and Mālwā and to which I have already referred in connection with the light which numismatics throws on political history. Here on their coins and in their inscriptions the actual ruler is invariably designated Mahākshatrapa and the heir-apparent merely Kshatrapa. Hence it becomes inexplicable how in the case of the Imperial Indo-Scythian dynasty the king and the prince-royal come to assume titles of precisely the same political grade. This knotty point I hope some one of you will be able to solve one day.

So much for one administrative puzzle presented by the study of numismatics. I will now place another before you. I shall here come to a somewhat later period, *viz.*, the Gupta period, and fix your attention on the coins of the founder of this dynasty. On the obverse are the figures of a king and his queen, who from the legends appear to be no other than Chandragupta I and his wife Kumāradevī, and on the reverse the legend has *Lichchhavayaḥ*, *i.e.* the Lichchhavis. What is the significance of these names? Those who are numismatists need not be told that as the name of the Lichchhavis occurs on the reverse, they had evidently become subordinate to Chandragupta I. But how did they come to occupy this subordinate position? Did Chandragupta conquer them? This does not appear to be possible, because his son Samudragupta calls himself with pride *Lichchhavi-dauhitra*, "the daughter's son of a Lichchhavi." This Lichchhavi father-in-law of Chandragupta could not have been a ruler of Nepāl as conjectured by Dr. Fleet. Before the conquest of Nepāl the Lichchhavis according to their tradition ruled at Pushpapura or Pāṭaliputra, and this is confirmed by one of the Nepāl inscriptions published by Pandit Bhagwanlal Indraji.[1] The Lichchhavis,

[1] *IA.*, IX, 178, v. 7.

you know, were an oligarchic tribe and consisted not of one but of many chiefs who ruled conjointly.[1] How could they have become subordinate to Chandragupta even through this matrimonial alliance? This is the real puzzle presented by Chandragupta's coins. Perhaps the solution is that he was already married to a Lichchhavi princess, and in some battle or through some such catastrophe all the Lichchhavi chiefs and their heirs were killed, leaving no male issue behind and leaving the whole state as patrimony to Kumāradevī, queen of Chandragupta. Kumāradevī thus through succession came to be the ruler of Pāṭaliputra and the surrounding Lichchhavi territory, and, being a Hindu wife, her husband was naturally associated with her in this rule. But that Kumāradevī was an actual ruler is seen from the fact that along with Chandragupta's her figure appears on the obverse of his coins. I do not claim any finality for the solution I have proposed, and I have no doubt that some one amongst you will suggest a better solution.

We now turn to the sphere of Historical Geography and see what light numismatics throws on it. In this connection the coins issued by the old republics of ancient India are

---

1 *CL.*, 167-8.

very useful. I shall give here two or three instances only.

We know that the Yaudheyas were an oligarchic tribe and are mentioned in inscriptions as being opposed to Rudradāman about 150 A.D. and to Samudragupta about 330 A.D. They have also been referred to in the Mahābhārata and by Pāṇini.[1] But the question arises: where are they to be located? It is scarcely necessary for me to remind you of Pāṇini's Sūtra *Janapade lup* (IV. 2. 81), according to which the name of a tribe or people serves also as the name of the country occupied by them. Hence when the question is asked: 'where are the Yaudheyas to be located,' it is also meant 'which was the province occupied by them?' Now, the answer to this question can be given only by their coins, *i.e.*, by taking into consideration the localities where the coins have been found. And we know that their coins 'are found in the Eastern Punjab, and all over the country between the Sutlej and Jumna Rivers. Two large finds have been made at Sonpath, between Delhi and Karnal.'[2] It is this knowledge supplied by numismatics that enabled Sir Alexander Cunningham to identify the Yaudheyas, rightly I think, with the Johiyas

---

[1] *CL.*, 165-7.

[2] *ASIR.*, XIV, 140; *CAI.*, 76.

settled along both banks of the Sutlej—which part is consequently known as Johiya-bār.

We know, again, from epigraphic records that the Mālavas were another tribe with oligarchic form of government. The present province of Mālwā which is in Central India was doubtless named after them when they were settled there. But when this province came to be called Mālwā after the Mālavas we do not exactly know, but certainly not till the Gupta period. In the time of Alexander, however, they were settled somewhere in the Punjab and have been referred to as the Malloi republic by the Greek historians who accompanied him.[1] Certainly the Mālavas must have migrated through the intermediate regions before they passed from the Punjab to Central India. But it may be asked : Is there any evidence as to what this intervening province was through which they moved southwards ? This evidence is furnished by their coins, which, as we know, have been picked up in large numbers in the south-east part of the Jaipur State called Nāgar-chāl in Rājputānā. As the coins here found range in date from circa 150 B.C. to circa 250 A.D., we may reasonably hold that in this period the Mālavas had established themselves in this province and must have been in occupation of that region when

---

[1] *CL.*, 158.

about 100 A.D. Ushavadāta, son-in-law of the Kshatrapa Nahapāna, defeated them,[1] as we learn from a Nāsik cave inscription. They were not then far distant from Pushkar near Ajmer.

The migrations of the Mālavas remind us of the migrations of another people which have been brought to light by their coins,—I mean the Śibis whose coins have been found in and near Nagarī not far from Chitorgaṛh in Rājputānā and who have been called not a Gaṇa but Janapada. Of course, from the Mahābhārata and also from an inscription we know that the Śibis originally belonged to the Punjab,[2] but coins show that some of them were settled in the Chitorgaṛh district shortly before Christ. It is curious, however, that the province so occupied by them is not called Śibi after them, but Madhyamikā, as is quite clear from their coin legend. In one of my lectures, I informed you that the province of Madhyamikā has been mentioned both in the Mahābhārata and Varāhamihira's *Bṛihat-saṁhitā*,[3] and that Madhyamikā was in reality the name of both the province and its principal town as Avanti and Ayodhyā no doubt were. The ccins thus enable us to identify the city of Madhyamikā with Nagarī, near Chitorgaṛh, which, as I have

[1] *IA.*, 1918, 75.

[2] *MASI.*, 123-4.

[3] *CL.*, 173, n. 3; *MASI.*, 124-5.

elsewhere shown, contains the ruins of a large town.[1] The significance of this identification will flash on you. You are aware that Patañjali in his *Mahābhāshya* gives two instances of *laṅ*, *viz.*, *aruṇad=Yavanaḥ Sāketam* and *aruṇad=Yavano Madhyamikām*, to show that the past event denoted by this *laṅ* must be such as is capable of being witnessed by the speaker. Patañjali thus evidently gives us to understand that the city of Madhyamikā was besieged by a Yavana or Greek prince shortly before he wrote. And naturally curiosity centred round the location of this Madhyamikā. This curiosity, we know, was gratified by the study of coins only, *i.e.*, by the occurrence of the name Madhyamikā on the coins of the Śibi Janapada. We thus see that this Madhyamikā can be no other than Nagarī itself, as far south as which place the Greek prince, whosoever he was, pushed forward in his expedition of conquest when Patañjali lived and wrote.

So much for the light which numismatics sheds on the ancient Geography of India. Let us now see what its utility is for the History of Religion. Religious history is of two kinds, *viz.*, socio-religious and mytho-religious. We shall first confine our attention, briefly, of course, to socio-religious history. The most important fact in this connection is the adoption of Hindu

---

[1] *MASI.*, 125 and ff.

religion by, and absorption into Hindu Society of, the foreign tribes which poured into India from time to time. This subject has been handled at full length by me in a paper entitled *Foreign Elements in the Hindu population.*[1] Epigraphic records are of great service in this respect, but numismatics is by no means far behind. What is noteworthy here is that not only did these foreigners embrace Hinduism, *i.e.*, Buddhism or Brahmanism, but that some of them also actually adopted Hindu names. Thus Gondophares, the founder of the Indo-Parthian dynasty, has one type of coins on the reverse of which figures Śiva holding a trident.[2] Similarly on at least two types of coins of Wema Kadphises, the second ruler of the Kushana family, we find Śiva bearing a trident, sometimes with his bull Nandin behind and sometimes with gourd and tiger skin.[3] Here then we have two foreign kings who had become worshippers of Śiva and consequently followers of Brahmanism. The case was, however, different with Wema Kadphises' successors, Kanishka, Huvishka and Vāsudeva. Here we notice great eclecticism practised by those Kushana rulers in the matter of religious faith. We find very few Greek, many Iranian, and only some Hindu divinities selected for

---

[1] *IA.*, 1911, 7 and ff.

[2] *BMCGSKI.*, lviii and 104; *JRAS.*, 1903, 285; *CCPML.*, 151-2.

[3] *BMCGSKI.*, 124 and ff.; *CCIM.*, 68; *CCPML.*, 183.

worship. This indicates a curious religious cast of mind with these Kushana sovereigns, and this sort of eclecticism we never find again in the religious history of India. But be it noted that this singular trait of religious mind evinced by these Kushanas in deducing a pantheon of their own by a selection from among the deities of various religions, which is of extreme importance for the religious history of any country, is made known to us for the first time not by epigraphy but numismatics only. Now, among the Indian divinities worshipped by these foreigners the most pre-eminent is, of course, Buddha, who, however, figures indubitably on the coins of Kanishka alone. There is nothing strange in this as Kanishka is looked upon as a patron of Buddhism. There can be no doubt in regard to the identity of Buddha on Kanishka's coins as he has been actually so named on them. And this is a very important piece of information and conveyed to us by numismatics only, because this is the earliest human representation of Buddha[1] known to us so far which can be assigned to the reign of any particular king. Although Kanishka was a devotee of Buddha, he had not given up the Kushana family worship of Śiva, which god

---

[1] Perhaps this goes back to the reign of his predecessor Kadaphes, because one coin-type on which his name is illegible but which on other grounds has been attributed to him, has on the obverse Buddha seated in conventional attitude (*JASB.*, 1897, 300; *CCPML*, 181).

also appears on some of his coins,[1] and also on those of Huvishka and Vāsudeva. The name of this god, as it appears on their coins, consists of four Greek letters O H Þ O, which has puzzled many numismatists. They are all convinced that the god so represented is no other than Śiva, but his name has baffled all their attempt at decipherment. Some numismatists equate it with Ugra (Śiva),[2] some see in it some connection with *ukshan* or *vṛisha*,[3] the bull of Śiva, and others take it to stand for Bhaveśa.[4] But none of these readings can be considered satisfactory, because the word *ukshan* or *vṛisha* by itself can hardly denote Śiva, and Bhaveśa and Ugra, although they are names of Śiva, can hardly be represented in sound by the four Greek characters. Now, the second of these four letters, as I have just said is H. Knowing as numismatists do how H is confounded with M in the Kushana period, I feel no hesitation in reading the letters to be O M Þ O, and taking them to stand for Umeśa.[5] The worship of Śiva seems to have been continued by the Scytho-Sassanians who succeeded

---

[1] *BMCGSKI.*, 132; *CCIM.*, 74; *CCPML.*, 187.

[2] *BMCGSKI.*, lxv.

[3] *Revue Numismatique*, 1888, 207; *NChr.*, 1892, 62; *JRAS.*, 1907, 1045, n.l.

[4] *JRAS.*, 1897, 323.

[5] The name of Umā occurs on a coin of Huvishka (*NChr.*, 1892., pl. XIII. 1) where M is twice written like H (*JRAS.*, 1897, 324).

the Kushanas. We thus have coins of Varahran V (A.D. 422-440), the reverse of which bears Śiva and bull.[1] This Śiva-bull type is afterwards found on the coins of only one king, *viz.*, Śaśāṅka, king of Gauḍa (A.D. 600-625).[2] But Śiva is not the only divinity that was worshipped. Other deities connected with him are found represented either jointly or severally on the coins of Huvishka, *viz.*, Skanda, Kumāra, Viśākha and Mahāsena. Nay, an instance is not wanting of even the bull of Śiva being worshipped by these foreigners. Thus on some coins of Mihirakula, the most powerful Hūṇa potentate, we have a bull-emblem of Śiva—with the legend *jayatu vṛishaḥ* on the reverse.[3]

As regards the adoption of Hindu names, there is but one instance among the foreign princes so far noted, *viz.*, Vāsudeva, successor of Huvishka. But if you turn to the Kshatrapa dynasty which held Surāshṭra and Mālwā, you will find that except two all the twenty-seven names of these rulers supplied to us by their coins are distinctly Hindu. The founder of this family was, of course, Chashṭana, and his father's name was Ysāmotika. Both these names are Scythic and therefore foreign. But immediately after Chasṭana we begin to get a

---

[1] *IC.*, pl. II, No. 15.

[2] *CCGD.*, 147.

[3] *CCIM.*, 236.

string of Hindu names, such as Jayadāman, Rudradāman and so forth, and as if to remind us that these Hindu names were borne by princes of alien extraction, we find immediately after Rudradāman the name Dāmaysada, about whose foreign origin no doubt can arise.

Let us now see whether a study of coins can prove itself useful in the sphere of mytho-religious history. A short while ago I told you that Gondophares and the Kushana rulers were devotees of Śiva and that this god was represented on the reverse of their coins. Evidently Śiva here figures as an object of worship. But how is Śiva worshipped now-a-days? Do the Hindus worship this deity under his man-like representation, *i.e.*, do they worship his image holding a trident and tiger-skin and standing near his bull, as we no doubt find him on the coins of these Indo-Scythian kings? Do they not invariably worship him under the form of Liṅga? Of course, images of Śiva as on these coins are by no means unknown at the present day or even as far back as the post-Gupta period, but certainly they are not now, and were never then, objects of worship. On the coins of these foreign rulers, however, the figure of Śiva has no significance except as an object of worship, and yet we find on them not a Liṅga but a regular representation of Śiva. This clearly shows that up to the time of the Kushana king Vāsudeva at any rate, Śiva worship had not come to be identified with Liṅga worship. Of course, from Patañjali's *Mahābhāshya* on Pāṇini's Sūtra, *jīvik-ārthe ch-āpaṇye* we learn that till his time, *i.e.*, the middle of the second century B.C., an image of Śiva and not phallus was made for worship.[1] But now we know that till the seventh century A.D., at any rate, Śiva in his human form continued to be worshipped, though already in the beginning of the Gupta period phallus worship was being foisted on the Śiva cult. And, in fact, the earliest representation of Liṅga that has been found in a Śaiva temple is at Guḍimallam in South India, and, on the grounds of plastic art, it cannot possibly be assigned to any date prior to the 4th century A.D. And even here, it is worthy of note, you do not see a mere Liṅga, but also a standing figure of Śiva attached to it in front[2] showing clearly that even in this period the representation of Śiva was not entirely forgotten and was not completely supplanted by Liṅga.[3] Another

---

[1] *JBBRAS.*, XVI, 208.

[2] T. A. Gopinatha Rao's *Elements of Hindu Iconography*, Vol. I., pt. I, p. 6.

[3] There is a sculpture originally found at Bhīṭā but now lying in the Lucknow Museum. Dr. Führer, who discovered it, apparently took it to be the capital of a column. Mr. R. D. Banerji, however, says that Dr. Führer did not pay much attention to the inscription on it, from a careful study of which it appears that the sculpture represents a Liṅga and that the date of the Liṅga on palaeographic evidence is the first century B. C. (ASI.-AR., 1909-10, 147-8). Now, in the first place,

very early representation of phallus is that supplied by the Liṅga stone found near the village of Karamḍāṇḍā and inscribed on the base.[1] The epigraph is dated 117 G.E.=436 A.D., and speaks of the Liṅga as Bhagavān Mahādeva, showing a clear identification of phallus with Śiva in this instance. But it must have taken sometime longer for the phallus to completely supersede and supplant, all over India, the human form of Śiva as an object of worship. For Śiva in his human representation certainly occurs, as I have said above, on the coins of Śaśāṅka who flourished in the first half of the seventh century A.D.

---

the characters cannot with certainty be proved to be earlier than those of the time of the Kushana king. Vāsudeva (circa 200 A.D.). Secondly, Mr. Banerji no doubt reads *l(iṁ)go* in his transcript, but the word is clearly *lago*, whatever that may mean. The late Dr. Bloch also read it *lago*, as Mr. Banerji informs us in a footnote. Thirdly, even taking the word to be *liṅgo* with Mr. Banerji and further correcting it into *liṅgaṁ*, it cannot denote the "phallic symbol of Śiva," because in inscriptions such an image is termed *Mahādeva*, as was rightly maintained by Bloch. Fourthly, what is meant by saying that "the *liṅga* of the sons of Khajahūti was dedicated by Nāgasiri," as Mr. Banerji's translation has it? If the sons of Khajahūti had caused the idol to be made, the construction would have been *liṅgaṁ kāritaṁ Khajahūti-putraiḥ pratishṭhāpitaṁ cha Vāsishṭhīputreṇa* etc. Fifthly, Mr. Banerji's opinion that the sculpture represents a Liṅga is based merely on the inscription which, as we have seen, does not speak of any Liṅga at all. He does not tell us that the sculpture looks like a Liṅga. Dr. Führer, on the other hand, looks upon it as the capital of a column, as we have seen. It is exceedingly desirable that some archaeologist should examine this sculpture carefully and tell us whether it has the form of a Liṅga.

[1] *EI.*, X. 70 & ff.

Connected with Śivā are the four gods, Skanda, Kumāra, Viśākha and Mahāsena. They are, however, regarded at present as only four different names of one and the same god, *viz.*, Kārtikeya. The well-known two verses of the Amarakosha, which include these names, are taken as giving seventeen names of this deity. In ancient times, however, these four names denoted four different gods. Of course, the passage from Patañjali's *Mahābhāshya*, which I have just referred to and which speaks of an image of Śiva made for worship, speaks also of Skanda and Viśākha in that connection. This indicates that images not only of Śiva but also of Skanda and Viśākha were made in Patañjali's time for worship. Here both Skanda and Viśākha have been mentioned. Certainly, if these two names had denoted but a single deity, Patañjali would have mentioned only one, but as he has used two names, it is clear that Skanda and Viśākha must denote two different gods. But let us see what coins teach us on this point. Those of you who have studied the Kushana coinage need not be told that we have two types of Huvishka's coins which are of great interest to us in this connection. One type bears on the reverse three gods who have been named Skanda, Kumāra and Viśākha, and another, four gods named Skanda, Kumāra, Viśākha and Mahāsena.[1] As

[1] *CCPML.*, 207.

all these names have each a figure corresponding to it, is it possible to doubt that Skanda, Kumāra, Viśākha and Mahāsena represent four different gods? The coins thus convey to us an important piece of mythological knowledge, which we do not yet know from any other source. Huviskha, most of you are aware, flourished in the second half of the second century A. D., and the Amarakosha is now-a-days being assigned to the 4th century A. D.[1] As the interval between the two is not very great, a doubt may naturally arise as to whether we are right in taking the two verses from the Amarakosha as giving us seventeen names of only one god, *viz.*, Kārtikeya. The two verses in question consist of four lines, and strange to say, none of these lines mentions more than one of the four gods Skanda, Kumāra, Viśākha and Mahāsena. Thus the first line has Mahāsena, the second Skanda, the third Viśākha, and the fourth Kumāra only. Had we not rather take each line separately and say that it really intends setting forth the different names of each one of these four gods instead of saying as we have been doing up till now that all the four lines together give seventeen names of one and the same god?

You will thus see what light is thrown and on what various aspects of the ancient history

---

[1] *IA.*, 1912, 216.

of India by the study of coins. But it is impossible, I am afraid, to perceive the full importance of numismatics unless we select coins of any particular class or period and find out what cumulative effect their critical study produces. I will show you what I mean by giving only one instance, *viz.*, the group of coins struck by the Greeks settled in and about north-west India. Of course, I have already referred to their extreme importance in respect of the political history of the Indo-Bactrian rule. I shall therefore refrain from doing so here. But the question that presents itself to us at the very outset and even before we can think of deducing their political history is: when and where did the Greeks first come in contact with the people of India? I know some of you may say: "Of course, in the time of Pāṇini," for does he not in one Sūtra teach us the formation of the word *Yavanānī* which is derived from *Yavana*, and which, as Kātyāyana tells us, signifies 'the writing of the Yavanas or Greeks?'" But this is just the misfortune of Pāṇini, for, because he mentions the word *Yavana* in his Sūtra, he is at once dragged down to the 4th century B.C.; *i.e.*, to a period after the invasion of Alexander. The internal evidence, which was adduced long ago by Goldstücker and Sir Ramkrishna Bhandarkar and which must perforce place Pāṇini at least in the 6th century B.C., is set aside, although it is of an irrefragible character, and most of the European scholars will not even entertain the idea that the Yavanas or Greeks might possibly have been on the borders of India long before Alexander, and that Pāṇini's reference to this people is thus perfectly compatible with the date assigned to him by Goldstücker and Sir Ramkrishna. In fact, I confess that the possibility of the Yavanas having come in contact with the people of India long prior to the time of Alexander had suggested itself to me when I first took up the study of the Aśoka inscriptions. Rock Edict XIII, as most of you must be aware, speaks of five Greek kings, whose kingdoms were, of course, outside India, at any rate, outside the dominions of Aśoka. But I am not referring here to the passage which contains the name of these Greek potentates. I am alluding here to that part of the edict which gives the list of those peoples whose countries were included in Aśoka's empire. And this list, be it noted, begins with these very Yonas, after whom are mentioned Kambojas, Gandhāras and so forth. The question here arises: Who were these Yavanas? Of course, they were Greeks. But where are they to be placed? It is no doubt tempting to say that they may have occupied Bactria which was certainly associated with Greek rule, at a somewhat later period, at any rate. In Aśoka's time

4

we know that Bactria was comprised in the Syrian empire of Antiochus Theos. We learn from the Greek historians, Trogus, Justin and Strabo, that it was Diodotus who first made Bactria independent. He was a Satrap of this province under Antiochus Theos, and it was after the death of this monarch that Diodotus took advantage of the disturbances that followed it and managed to make himself independent. It is therefore impossible to locate the Yonas of Rock Edict XIII in Bactria, because this edict was promulgated when Antiochus Theos was living, his name being actually specified therein. Which country, then, did these Yonas occupy? Of course, it must have bordered on Gandhāra, which is mentioned immediately after it in Aśoka's inscription. And I suspect that it has to be identified with Aria or Arachosia which were the two provinces ceded by Seleucuos to Chandragupta and which must have been inherited intact by Aśoka. I admit it is not possible to locate these Yonas exactly, but this much is certain that they were outside the kingdom of Antiochus Theos, and lived in Aśoka's empire in a territory adjoining Gandhāra but outside India. But when could they have come and settled there? Did they come with Alexander? No, this is not possible, because the Macedonian conqueror did not leave behind him any permanent settlements in or near India.

Of course, he may have left some Greek garrisons, but certainly a province is not named after the race of garrisoned soldiers. It is only when a tribe or people comes in such terrific masses as to outnumber the original inhabitants that it gives its name to the province so occupied by them. We have many such instances, *e.g.*, of the Ābhīras, Gurjaras and so on.[1] The idea of a mere garrison imparting the name of its raçe to the country where it is stationed is, I am afraid, utterly inadmissible, if not even ludicrous. In all likelihood, the Yavanas of Rock Edict XIII must have come and settled in large numbers in some outlying province of India long before Alexander. But if we assume that the Yavanas had their colony in a territory conterminous to India, they must have exercised some sort of political independence and for at least some period, and have we, you may naturally ask, got any evidence to that effect? And this question numismatics is, I think, in a position to answer in the affirmative. Coins, similar to those of the earliest type of Athens, are known to have been collected from the north-west frontiers of India. They bear head of Athena on the obverse and owl on the reverse.[2] And the question must naturally arise: Why are they to be found in the frontier provinces of

---

[1] *JBBRAS*, XXI, 430 and ff.

[2] *NChr.*, XX, 191.

India? It is no doubt possible to say that these *owls* of Athens, as this type of coinage is called, were carried to India in the course of commerce.[1] Similar *owls* have also been picked up in Southern Arabia Felix.[2] But none of the *owls* found in the east are of the types known from Athens. In the case of this Semitic country, again, it is not impossible to say that they may have travelled there as a result of commercial intercourse, because they are generally countermarked on the obverse with Sabaean letters or are scratched with a Sabaean monogram on the reverse. When a foreign money for the first time comes into circulation along with the native coinage of a country, all the new specimens are tested, and those, which are found not deficient in weight or quality of metal, are sanctioned by marking them with an official stamp, which may consist of a single letter or symbol. These official stamps are no doubt noticeable on the *owls* of Athens brought to light in South Arabia. But they are conspicuous by their absence on those recovered on the frontiers of India. It cannot be doubted that the practice of countermarking foreign coinage in circulation was observed in or near India also, for we do know that the silver Persian sigloi which were current

[1] *IC.*, p. 3. §9.

[2] G. F. Hill's *The Ancient Coinage of Southern Arabia* (Reprint from the *Proceedings of the British Academy*, Vol. VII), pp. 2-3.

in the Punjab bear distinctly Indian countermarks.[1] When, therefore, no countermarks are traceable on the *owls* of Athens picked up from the frontier region of India, it is not reasonable to say that they were brought there with the expansion of commerce. The natural inference must be that they were native to some outlying district of India which was peopled by the Yavanas or Greeks. And as the original *owls* of Athens have been assigned to *circa* 594-560 B.C.,[2] a Greek colony, it is possible to infer, may have been established near India about 550 B.C.[3] There can, after all, be nothing strange in Pāṇini flourishing in the 6th century B.C. and in his referring also to Yavanānī, the writing of the Greeks. In fact, if it is not admitted that the Greeks had a settlement near India before Alexander, how is it possible, I ask, to unravel the enigma about the coins of Sophytes? Sophytes, you know, ruled over a province somewhere in the Western Punjab when Alexander invaded India, and as he acknowledged speedy submission to the Macedonian emperor, he was re-instated in his kingdom. Now, we have found some coins, which bear his head on the obverse and a cock and

---

[1] *JRAS.*, 1895, 874 and ff.

[2] Hill's *Historical Greek Coins*, 11.

[3] For the extreme probability of a similar Roman settlement at or near Madura in the Madras Presidency, see *JRAS.*, 1904, 613-5.

his name in Greek character on the reverse. When could he have struck these coins? This is the most puzzling question to answer. Did he strike them after the death of Alexander but before the Punjab was subjugated by Chandragupta? Then it is very strange that we do not see the bust of Alexander instead of his. For up to B.C. 306, *i.e.*, till the extinction of the old royal line of Macedonia, we find that all the generals of Alexander retain the name and bust of Alexander on their coins, and if Sophytes was no better and perhaps even worse in point of political power than these generals, does it not look the height of presumption for him to have his own name and bust on the coins instead of those of Alexander who was doubtless his overlord? And if it is the height of presumption to have his name and bust on coins, if they are supposed to be struck after the death of Alexander, would it not be sheer folly on his part if he issued them when Alexander was actually alive and in the Punjab? I am afraid, the only way to get over this difficulty is to suppose that Sophytes struck his coins before Alexander invaded India and before he lost his independence. Now, if Sophytes was an Indian by extraction, how is it possible to account for the presence of a bust and the employment of the Greek character before the Macedonian conquest of the Punjab? This is simply inconceivable.

The only explanation that is plausible is that he was a Greek prince in India before the advent of Alexander. I know Sophytes is not considered to be a Greek name. It has been taken to be identical with the Sanskrit Saubhūti.[1] But there is nothing strange in a Greek taking a Hindu name immediately before the Maurya period, if another Greek, shortly after, *i.e.*, in Aśoka's time, adopts a Persian name, *viz.*, Tushāspa.

But if the Greeks really conquered some region near the north-west frontiers of India and were settled there, as no doubt numismatic considerations lead us to conclude, is there any reference to such a fact in any one of the accounts drawn up by the Macedonian historians of India about the time of Alexander's invasion? If the Greeks really established a colony in a border province of India, it is inconceivable that such a thing which would be of supreme interest to a Greek should be ignored by any historian of Alexander's time. Do we then, as a matter of fact, find any reference to it in the work of any Greek historian? This is the natural question that must arise here and which you will no doubt expect me to tackle even though I may have to deviate strictly from the subject of to-night's lecture. And I am glad to say that

[1] Rapson's *Ancient India*, 162-3; *CCIM.*, 7.

there are two passages in the Fifth Book of Arrian's work which in my opinion answer this question and thus corroborate the numismatic evidence.[1] The passages in question, to which Mr. Hemchandra Raychaudhuri was the first to draw my attention, give a description of the city and people of Nysa which was situated between the Kophen and the Indus. The deputies of Nysa, who waited upon Alexander, themselves told the Macedonian monarch that **their city was founded by Dionysos** as he was returning to the shores of Greece after conquering the Indian nation and that he called it Nysa after the name of his nurse Nysa, and in proof of their statement that Dionysos was their founder adduced the fact that ivy which grew nowhere else in the land of the Indians grew in their city. In fact, anybody who carefully reads these passages will be convinced that Dionysos here is a real Hellenic deity and not any Hindu god in Hellenic garb and that the account clearly points to Nysa having been a Greek colony.

Let us now look at the coins of the Indo-Bactrian Greeks from the religious point of view. You will perhaps wonder what new thing can possibly be taught by this class of coins.

---

[1] McCrindle's *Ancient India : its Invasion; by Alexander the Great*, 79-80. For an ancient Greek burial ground, see *IA.*, 1909, 144.

And you may naturally ask: What new contribution these coins can possibly make to the knowledge of Hellenic pantheon which we already possess from more direct and exhaustive sources? Let us, however, see whether it is possible to approach the study of these coins from a new angle of vision. If Sophytes was a Greek of the time of Alexander and yet he adopted a Hindu name, is it not possible to say that some of the Indo-Bactrian kings must have embraced Hindu religion? Or if you want to leave Sophytes out of account, do we not know that during the regime of Antialkidas when the Indo-Bactrian rule was in the heyday of its glory, his very ambassador Heliodorus, a Greek, had become a Bhāgavata, a devotee of Vāsudeva? How is it then possible to think that none of the Indo-Bactrian kings was a Hindu? Is it not therefore possible to study their coins more closely and from this view-point? In this connection, allow me to invite your attention to the square bronze coins of Eucratides. The deity figuring on the reverse has been taken to be Zeus seated on throne who holds a wreath and a palm branch and has fore-part of elephant in front of him.[1] There is also a Kharoshthī inscription on the reverse, which reads *Kaviśiye nagara-devata* and means "the city-deity of

[1] *JRAS.*, 1905, 783 & ff.

Kāpiśī." Now, Kāpiśī was a Hindu town and has been referred to in one of Pāṇini's Sūtras as a place where good wine was brewed.[1] Evidently, therefore, the divinity figuring on the coin is a Hindu one, being the *nagara-devatā* of Kāpiśī, and yet it has been so figured on the coin that it can be easily mistaken for a Greek deity and has actually been mistaken for Zeus by the numismatists, as we have seen. The term *nagara-devatā* occurs on another coin also, which unfortunately cannot be assigned to any king as the legends on it have not been preserved whole and entire. On the obverse is a goddess with the Kharoshṭhī legend [*Pa*]*khalavadi-devada*,[2] which has been taken to mean the tutelary divinity of Pushkalāvatī. Pushkalāvatī also was a Hindu city, and yet we find that the goddess on this coin wears Greek dress and a mural crown which is the emblem of a Greek civic deity. The natural inference from a study of these coins is that mere Greek dress and emblems do not stamp a deity as necessarily a Hellenic one and that a Hindu divinity may appear under Hellenic garb on Indo-Bactrian coins. The Greeks were notorious for identifying foreign deities with their own so long as there were any characteristics in common. For

---

[1] IV. 2. 99.

[2] *JRAS.*, 1905, 787.

do we not know that Megasthenes, *e.g.*, calls Kṛishṇa or rather Balarāma of Mathurā, Herakles, and Śiva of the hills, Dionysos? Nay, that some of the deities occurring on the coins of the Indo-Bactrian Greek princes may not be Hellenic, though they are invested with Hellenic attributes, was suspected long ago by Percy Gardner. "On coins of Demetrius," says this eminent numismatist, "Artemis is sometimes radiate, on coins of Agathocles Zeus bears in his hand the three-headed Hekate, Herakles crowns himself with a wreath, Pallas appears in short skirts, and many other such strange forms of Greek deities appear. To search out the reasons of these variations of type, reasons to be found probably in many instances in the influence of local Indian or Persian legend or belief, would be a very attractive task, and not hopeless, considering the data furnished us by the legends of the gold Indo-Scythic coins. The earliest of the clearly Indian types to make its appearance is a dancing-girl, wearing long hanging ear-rings and oriental trousers, on the money of Pantaleon and Agathocles. As we come to a later period, non-Hellenic types, or types in which there is a non-Hellenic element, gradually make their way on the coins. On coins of Philoxenus and Telephus we find a radiate figure of a sun-god, holding a long sceptre. On those of Amyntas and Hermaeus we find the head of a deity wearing

Phrygian cap, whence issue rays."[1] I am sorry I had to quote this long extract here, but as Percy Gardner is looked upon as a very great authority on this subject, his opinion must be considered to be invaluable. And you have just seen what that opinion is. He clearly admits that some types of Greek deities are fantastic even according to the Hellenic standard and that some contain an unmistakable non-Hellenic element. It is a matter of regret that no numismatist has gone farther than where Percy Gardner left this line of inquiry, but what I have said is enough to show to you that the Indo-Bactrian Greeks were by no means slow to be influenced by Indian and other religious beliefs with which they came in contact. The exact character and extent of this influence can be determined only by a critical study of their coins, and the results of such a study, I have no doubt, will form an important contribution to the religious history of India, if not of the world.

---

[1] *BMCGSKI.*, Intro., lvii-lviii.

LECTURE II

ANTIQUITY OF COINAGE IN INDIA

I believe, you still remember the words which the President of the last Oriental Conference used in regard to the mentality of the European and the Indian scholar towards Oriental subjects. "The Indian's tendency," said he, "may be towards rejecting foreign influence on the development of his country's civilization and to claim high antiquity for some of the occurrences in its history. On the other hand, the European scholar's tendency is to trace Greek, Roman or Christian influence at work in the evolution of new points and to modernize the Indian historical and literary events." It is not possible to determine how far these words are true of the Indian scholars in regard to the ancient Indian numismatics, because there is hardly any one amongst them yet who has seriously devoted himself to this subject, but it must be admitted that they are true of some of the European scholars who were or are looked upon as authorities on this subject. Their attempt seems to have been unconsciously to prove that the invention of coinage was not indigenous to India and that the Indians learnt the art of stamping money either from the Babylonians or from the Greeks, and that again certainly not prior to B.C. 600 or 700. Thus James Prinsep, to whom must always go the honour of having unravelled the most ancient Indian alphabet, the Brāhmī *lipi*, thought that the Hindus derived their knowledge of coinage from the Greeks of Bactria. And although afterwards he had to admit that the Hindus had an indigenous currency of precious metals, he persisted in at least maintaining that from the time the Greeks entered India "may be assumed the adoption of a *die-device*, or of coined money properly so called, by the Hindus."[1] And as Prinsep was Assay Master of the Calcutta Mint, his words naturally carried great weight. And it is not strange if we find that H. H. Wilson, the author of the *Ariana Antiqua*, also indulged in surmise, and asserted that it was "likely that the currency of the country consisted chiefly, if not exclusively, of lumps of gold and silver not bearing any impression, until the Hindus had learned the usefulness of money from their Bactrian neighbours, and from their commerce, especially with Rome."[2] At the time when Prinsep and Wilson wrote, there were two other numismatists, both of them Englishmen, Alexander Cunningham

---

[1] *JASB.*, I. 394; IV. 626.

[2] *AA.*, 404.

and Edward Thomas, who, however, held the opposite view, and maintained the existence of an indigenous Indian coinage. But their arguments, forcible and cogent though they were, were left unheeded, and the tendency of assigning a later date and tracing almost everything Indian that is good or original to a foreign source, which is so natural to some European writers, re-asserted itself, probably with greater vigour. Thus James Kennedy holds that the punch-marked coins, or the Kārshāpaṇas as they were known to the ancient Hindus, which form the most ancient money in India, were copied from Babylonian originals after the opening of maritime trade in the sixth century B.C.[1] V. A. Smith's view is substantially the same. In his article on Numismatics, which he contributed to the *Imperial Gazetteer*, he says as follows: "The introduction into India of the use of coins, that is to say, metallic pieces of definite weight authenticated as currency by marks recognised as a guarantee of value, may be ascribed with much probability to the seventh century B.C., when foreign maritime trade seems to have begun. There is reason to believe that the necessities of commerce with foreign merchants were the immediate occasion for the adoption by the Indian people of a metallic currency as well as of alphabetical writing."[2]

---

[1] *JRAS.*, 1898, p. 279 & ff.

[2] *IG.*, II. 135.

In his *Catalogue of Coins in the Indian Museum, Calcutta*, he gives a later date to the earliest coinage of India, the earliest type of the Kārshāpaṇas being assigned by him to 500 or 600 B.C.[1]

Such, in short, are the theories held by most of the European numismatists in regard to the origin and antiquity of the Indian coinage. The view that the knowledge of the stamped or die-struck coins the Hindus obtained from the Bactrian Greeks, which was originally started by James Prinsep, is no longer countenanced by numismatists of any repute. As early as 1853 when, Sir, then Mr., E. C. Bayley was Deputy Commissioner of the Kangra District in the Punjab, were discovered a number of silver coins "comprising specimens of Antimachus II, Philoxenes, Lysias, Antialkidas, and Menander, together with a few punch-marked pieces, the last being *much worn*, whilst all the Greek coins were comparatively *fresh*."[2] Evidence of a more convincing nature has been furnished by a find of coins made in Sir John Marshall's excavations at Taxila during the cold season of the year 1912-13. In the Bir Mound, the earliest of the three cities till then excavated by him there, he lighted upon a small hoard in the shape of one hundred and seventy-five punch-marked coins along with

[1] *CCIMC.*, 133.

[2] *N Chr.*, XIII (1873), 209; CAI., 54.

a gold coin of Diodotus struck in the name of Antiochus II of Syria.[1] It will thus be seen that the hoard belongs to a period when Diodotus was still a Satrap of Antiochus and before he declared the independence of Bactria. As the punch-marked coins of this deposit are thus of a time when Bactria was still subordinate to the Seleukidan power, it is not possible to assert now that the Hindus learnt the art of coinage from their Bactrian Greek neighbours. Even numismatic considerations pointed to the same inevitable conclusion, as was contended long ago by Alexander Cunningham. "If the Hindus had derived their knowledge of coinage from the Greeks, the types, shape, and standard of all their money would have been Greek."[2] The Bactrian Greek coins are round in form, conform to the Attic standard, and contain invariably a bust on the obverse and a Hellenic deity on the reverse. The earliest Hindu coins, on the other hand, are mostly square in form, correspond to any but the Attic standard, and, in point of type, have never shown any bust or any Hellenic divinity on any one of their sides. Besides, they are utterly without inscriptions which are invariably found on Bactrian Greek coins. In these circumstances, to say that the Hindus are indebted to the Bactrian Greeks for

---

[1] ASI.-AR., 1912-13, pp. 41-2.

[2] NChr., XIII (1873), 212.

the art of stamping money is a mere gratuitous supposition unwarranted by any facts or rather opposed to all facts. It is no wonder, therefore, if the modern followers of Prinsep and Wilson have given up this assailable position, and are now taking their stand on the ground that the art of coin-making was adopted by the imitative Hindus, somewhat earlier, *i.e.*, between 500 and 700 B.C., but doubtless from some foreigners, possibly the Babylonians. You may perhaps ask whether Cunningham and Thomas, who, representing the other view, have any successors at present just as Prinsep and Wilson have Kennedy and Smith, and I may therefore inform you that amongst the modern numismatists Prof. Rapson is the only one who holds that the most ancient coinage of India was developed independently of any foreign influence.[1] In regard to their date, however, he says that its earliest specimens are probably as early as the beginning of the 4th century B.C. only.[2]

I confess, I cannot possibly understand how Kennedy and Smith can bring themselves to regard the Kārshāpaṇas, the earliest coinage of India, as a foreign importation. Both again go to the extent of saying that the Hindus adopted the art of coin-making just as they learnt the usefulness of alphabet—from foreign country. This is,

---

[1] JRAS., 1895, 869 & ff.

[2] IC., 2.

indeed, a most astounding assertion. Of course, there was something to be said in favour of those who held that the Brāhmī, the oldest Indian alphabet, was derived from the Semitic script, as no doubt was contended by Weber and Bühler. We had both Brāhmī and Semitic alphabets before us for our scrutiny. We could very well see that there were many characters which bore close resemblance to each other, and were intended to denote the same sound. Again, it was almost conclusively shown that the Brāhmī like all Semitic alphabets, was originally written from right to left. Besides, the earliest Semitic script was definitely known to be earlier than the earliest form of the Brāhmī *lipi*. When, therefore, Bühler wrote on this subject, he was certainly right in maintaining that the Brāhmī was derived from the Semitic script, though, as I showed you last year, we have now to abandon this theory in the light of the evidence furnished by certain pre-historic artifacts. But what are the grounds for saying that the Hindus adopted their metallic currency from foreign source, as is no doubt asserted by Kennedy and Smith? Have they found any coins outside India of a period prior to 600 or 700 B.C. and of a type closely corresponding to the Kārshāpaṇas? Is there any evidence at all to show that there was foreign coinage, of a date anterior to 600 or 700 B.C. the earliest date assigned by them to the Kārshāpaṇas, which through identity or at any rate extreme similarity of type can rightly be called to be their prototype? I confess I am not aware of any such foreign coinage, and carefully as I have read the articles written by Kennedy and Smith on this subject, I do not find that they ever describe what sort of foreign coinage this was or even attempt to adduce any shred of evidence to show that such a coinage at all existed outside India. In these circumstances is it not absurd to asseverate that the Hindus learnt the use of coinage from foreigners? Does it not clearly indicate that such an *ipse dixit* has been prompted by nothing but the propensity of attributing everything useful or clever in Indian art to an extraneous origin? I emphatically and without any fear of contradiction maintain that the Kārshāpaṇa coinage, which is the earliest metallic currency whose specimens are found in India, has not yet been definitely proved to be of foreign origin.

To find out, however, whether there was any foreign influence on the earliest metallic currency of India, we must discuss the question: to what earliest period the art of coin-making in India is traceable. The question can be satisfactorily answered only by ransacking our literature, sacred and profane, Brahmanic and Buddhist, and finding out what classes of coins were prevalent at different periods before 400 B.C. which is the earliest date assigned by Prof. Rapson to the Kārshāpaṇas.

Now, if we take up Pāṇini's *Ashṭādhyāyī* which is useful not only for the study of Sanskrit grammar but also for constructing the social, religious and economic history of India, we find that in *adhyāya* V and *pāda* 1 he mentions certain affixes which have the sense of *tena krītaṁ*, *i.e.* "purchased with this price" and *tad=arhati*, *i.e.* "which deserves that." You can at once perceive that here is a section which must throw some light on the economic condition of India in Pāṇini's time and the various media of exchange then prevalent. And, as a matter of fact, this natural expectation is more than fully realised through a study of these Sūtras. We are not, however, here concerned with a detailed specification of these media of exchange. Our present object is merely to ascertain whether there are any references to the use of coins in Pāṇini's work, and if so, what kinds are mentioned. And somewhat startling as it may appear, we notice that Pāṇini refers to at least seven kinds of coins. Not only does he speak of the Kārshāpaṇas but also of Nishkas, Śatamānas and so forth. Pāṇini, as I have repeatedly told you, has to be assigned to the middle of the 6th century B.C. at the latest. And if seven different types of metallic currency were prevalent in India about 550 B.C., the beginning of the art of coin-making in this country must be placed earlier than 700 B.C.

But I can very well imagine some sense of doubt crossing your mind. I have no doubt said that Pāṇini flourished about 550 B.C. Prof. Goldstücker and Sir Ramkrishna Bhandarkar would place him even earlier. But as I have told you in my last lecture, this view is not shared by the European scholars in general. The argument about the antiquity of Indian coinage, which may be based upon the study of Pāṇini's Sūtras as I have done just now, will, I am afraid, not carry conviction to them, as they drag Pāṇini down to 350 B.C. We must, therefore, base our argument on that section of Indian literature, about the early date of which there is a general consensus of opinion among European scholars. And what other works can present themselves to our mind in this connection than the Jātakas or Buddha's Birth Stories which form an important part of Buddhist literature ? The Jātaka stories may not perhaps constitute the earliest class of this literature, but certain it is that they represent a social and political condition prior to the rise of Buddhism and belonging to the sixth or even seventh century B.C. This is the opinion not of Indian antiquarians but of European scholars, such as Bühler and Prof. Rhys Davids.[1] Let us, therefore,

---

[1] Bühler (IS., III. 16 & ff) refers the Pāli Buddhist Canon "to the fifth and possibly to the sixth century B.C."; and as he says that

see what the Jātaka tales teach us on this point, *i.e.* whether they speak of any class or classes of coins which were current in India at the early period.

Now, any one who carefully studies Pāṇini's Sūtras and the Jātaka stories cannot but be impressed by the fact that both depict ancient India of practically the same period. It is not, therefore, surprising if we find the same classes of coins referred to in both. But Pāṇini's *Ashṭādhyāyī*, just because it consists of aphorisms, cannot be expected to throw much light on this subject beyond the mere mention of the denominations of coins. The case is, however, different in regard to the Buddhist Jātakas. As they portray social and economic India of the 7th century B.C., it is here that we can clearly see what part, insignificant or important, stamped metallic currency played in the manifold transactions of the people at that early period. Let us, in the first place, see whether there was any gold currency in India at that time. Of course, as India was the land of gold in those days at least, we must naturally expect some sort of gold coinage to have been then prevalent. And we certainly find that our expectations are

---

the Jātaka stories are loans from "the old pre-Buddhistic national tradition of India" and that the state of civilisation described in them "is in various respects primitive," the life portrayed in them must be assigned to the seventh, at the latest the sixth, century B.C. For Rhys Davids' views, see *Buddhist India*, 207-8.

not unfounded. For we read of at least three classes of gold coinage in the Jātaka literature. And as gold is the most precious metal of which coins can be manufactured, it is only in connection with hoards of money, munificent gifts and so forth that we find gold coins mentioned. Thus the Kuhaka Jātaka[1] gives us an amusing story of a scamp of an ascetic who goes to a village and lives in a hermitage built by a local Kuṭuṃbika or farmer. Taking the ascetic to be a model of goodness, the farmer brings his hundred *nishkas* of gold to the hermitage and there buries them, requesting him to keep watch over them. Confiding in the pious protestations of the hermit, the farmer goes off, but the former covertly removes the gold and buries it in the wayside. The very next day the ascetic takes leave of the farmer, but returns shortly after to return a straw from the farmer's roof which has stuck in his matted hair but which does not belong to him. This over-manifestation of moral sensitiveness arouses the suspicion of a shrewd trader who has halted on the outskirts of the village and who forthwith sees the farmer and warns him. Away they hasten in hot pursuit, catch the rascal, and kick and cuff him till he shows to them where he hid the gold. The trader, who is the Bodhisattva of this story, rebukes the ascetic, saying : "So a hundred

[1] Jāt. I, 375 & ff.

Nishkas did not trouble your conscience so much as that straw." Here then a specific class of coins—gold coins—is mentioned, *viz.* Nishkas, for the valuation of a rich farmer's hoarding. Only two references to Nishkas may be given out of the many which I was able to trace in the Jātakas. Some of you are pretty well conversant with the Vessantara Jātaka, which, among other things, tells us how Vessantara, King of Śibi, who had retired to a forest, gives over his son and daughter completely to a Brāhmaṇ called Jūjaka.[1] Of course, the children are reluctant to go, and he comforts them by saying : " Son Jāli, if you wish to become free, you must pay the Brāhmaṇ a thousand Nishkas. But your sister is very beautiful ; if any person of low birth should give the Brāhmaṇ so and so much to make her free, he would break her birthright. None but a king can give all things by the hundred ; therefore if your sister would be free, let her pay the Brāhmaṇ a hundred male and a hundred female slaves together with elephants, horses, bulls and Nishkas, all a hundred each." Thus did he price the children and comfort them, and taking water in his waterpot he poured it out, giving the Brāhmaṇ this precious gift of his children. Here we have a father before us, putting a price upon his children ; and as the latter are of the royal blood, naturally this

[1] *Ibid.*, VI, 546. 28 ; 547. 6.

price has to be the heaviest, and the coins to appraise it must necessarily be of the highest value. The Nishkas here specified must, therefore, represent the highest order of gold coins. We now turn to a third Jātaka, the Great Being of which story is a snake-king called Champeyya who allows himself to be caught by a snake-charmer for his good. By making the snake perform to the crowd of a frontier village the snake-charmer earns as much as one thousand Kārshāpaṇas in one single day.[1] Desire of further gain impels him to go to the capital-town, Vārāṇasī. While the performance to the local king is going on, the wife of the snake-king suddenly makes her appearance and offers a handsome ransom, one of the numerous items of which is one hundred Nishkas.[2] In this Jātaka we find two classes of coins specified, *viz.* the Kārshāpaṇas and Nishkas. The first evidently are the silver and the second the gold money of the country of Kāśi.

It is, however, a mistake to suppose that Nishkas were the only class of gold coins known to the Jātaka literature. Not unfrequently we meet with an expression in which the words *hiraṇya* and *suvarṇa* are associated together. Thus the Bhūridatta Jātaka gives us another tale of a snake-king tamed by a snake-charmer

---

[1] *Ibid.*, IV. 458. 6.

[2] *Ibid.*, 460. 28 ; 461. 7 & 10.

who amassed a fortune by making him assume various appearances and exhibit dancing powers. At the very first performance that he gave in a village, the people, we are told, were so pleased that they heaped on him *hiraṇya*, *suvarṇa*, *vastra*, *alaṁkāra* and the like.[1] Of course, *vastra* and *alaṁkāra* mean 'garments' and 'ornaments' respectively. But what about *hiraṇya* and *suvarṇa*? For both signify 'gold,' and consequently one of these words becomes superfluous. On the other hand, *suvarṇa* denotes a specific kind of gold coins, which the other word, *viz.* *hiraṇya*, does not. It is truc that Suvarṇa denotes a certain weight as well as a gold coin of this weight, and it is no doubt possible to suppose that in this particular Jātaka story, the word *suvarṇa* means merely gold bullion of this weight. But according to this supposition, *suvarṇa*, like the other word, *viz.* *hiraṇya*, would signify gold only, and thus there remains no distinction between the two. Are we not therefore compelled to infer that *suvarṇa* in this as in other places where it is associated with *hiraṇya* must stand not for 'gold' but a 'type of gold coins'? But this is not all. For in the

[1] *Ibid.*, VI. 186. 3. The phrase *hiraññа-suvaṇṇa* occurs also in Jāt. VI. 69. 18, which is translated by 'gold and coin' by Cowell and Rouse (p. 38). The same phrase is met with in Kauṭilya's Arthaśāstra (p. 243) also but in its Sanskrit form, and is rendered by Mr. Shama Sastri as 'bar gold and coined gold' (p. 305). Compare also JRAS., 1901, p. 879.

Jātaka literature we read of gold coins of a still smaller denomination. I have been able to trace at least two references to a type of gold coins called Suvarṇa-Māshaka. Thus in the Udaya-Jātaka we are introduced to Udayabhadra and Udayabhadrā, who are brother and sister and yet become husband and wife. They are the king and queen of the Kāśi kingdom. Udayabhadra dies, and becomes Śakra in the Heaven of the Thirty-three (*Tāvatiṁsa-bhavana*). And he comes to the mortal world one day to tempt his former wife with riches, by, we are told, lavishing encomium on her beauty and holding before her a golden dish replete with Suvarṇa-Māshakas.[1] Again, in the Saṁkhapāla-Jātaka we have a third instance of a snake-king being captured, this time, however, by a party of sixteen men. A rich landowner, who happens to pass that way, sees the Bodhisattva in great agony, and, struck with compassion, releases him by making handsome gifts to those lewd fellows amongst which prominent mention is made of the Suvarṇa-Māshakas.[2] But what is a Suvarṇa-Māshaka, you may naturally ask me here? I may have something to tell you about it in my next lectures, but here it will be sufficient to state that *māsha* is a unit in the weight system of Indian coinage which differs in weight according as the coin is of gold, silver

---

[1] Jāt., IV. 106. 1; 107. 17.

[2] *Ibid.*, V. 164. 15-6.

or copper. And while, as a rule, *māsha* denotes the weight, Māshaka denotes a coin of this weight. A Suvarṇa-Māshaka is, therefore, a gold coin which is equal to one *māsha* in weight according to the standard of gold coinage. And in the first of the two instances here quoted we have seen that Udayabhadra holds in front of his wife a plate filled with Suvarṇa-Māshakas, which, just because we are not told how many they were, cannot denote pieces of gold bullion but gold coins only,—such as were ready at hand and could be got hold of at any time for waving them round a person. As the plate is said to have been filled with Suvarṇa-Māshakas, it follows that they were all distinct pieces, so that each one of them could be called a Suvarṇa-Māshaka, and that each piece weighed one *māsha*. And are we to suppose that in this instance gold bullion was so adroitly chopped off, and just on the spur of the moment, that every bit weighed exactly one *māsha* and could thus be a separate piece by itself? This is simply absurd. We thus perceive that in ancient India of the sixth or perhaps of the seventh century B. C. no less than three types of gold coins were current. Of the lowest value was the Māshaka, of a higher denomination was the Suvarṇa, and of a still higher denomination, the Nishka.

There was yet another class of coins which is frequently referred to in the Jātaka stories.

I mean the Kārshāpaṇa about which most of you must have already heard. I do not wish to say much here about this type as the whole of my next lecture will be devoted to this subject. The Kārshāpaṇa, as we read of it in the Jātaka literature, was of three varieties according as it was of gold, silver and copper. Gold Kārshāpaṇa, however, is seldom referred to, and the common types of Kārshāpaṇa that we hear of are either silver or copper. How extensive and deep the circulation of this type of money was in all the strata of the society of the seventh century B. C. is clear even from a cursory study of the Jātaka tales, but this we shall see in the next lecture.

I am afraid we cannot stop here but must proceed further to find out whether there are any references to metallic currency in literature of a still earlier date than that of the Jātakas. You must have already guessed that it is the Vedic literature that I am here alluding to. No doubt, even here there is perceptible the tendency of some European scholars to drag down the various compositions of this literature to as late a period as possible. But even then it must be admitted that they have not been able to place them later than the age represented by the Jātakas. If we can, therefore, trace any mention of coined money in the Vedic literature, we can conclusively say that the use of this money was known to India long long prior to 600 or 700 B.C. Let us therefore see whether the works comprising this literature make mention of the metallic currency. Some of you probably know that Kātyāyana's *Śrauta-sūtra* contains a reference to a coin called Śatamāna. It is curious that there is no mention of this class of coins anywhere in the Buddhist works, though the name occurs in a Pāṇini's *sūtra*[1] and Kātyāyana's *vārtika*,[2] showing clearly that Śatamāna was known till the Maurya period. The *Śrauta-sūtra* of Kātyāyana, in the chapter entitled the *Rājasūya-nirūpaṇam*, refers to the Śatamāna coin in three consecutive Sūtras.[3] But this *Śrauta-sūtra* probably is of the same period as the Jātakas, and it may consequently be argued that it does not take us anterior to the time we have reached on the strength of these Buddhist Birth Stories. We must, therefore, go to Vedic compositions which are prior in date to this Sūtra. The class of writings, which are of an immediately prior period to the Śrauta-Sūtras are, of course, the Upanishads. The only coin name that we meet with in these works is Nishka which occurs thrice in the Chhāṃdogya.[4] But if we correctly interpret the passages of this Upanishad, the word *nishka* in them must be taken

---

[1] V. 1. 27.

[2] On Pāṇini's V. 1. 29.

[3] XV. 181-3.

[4] IV. 2. 1-3.

to signify "a necklace" and not "a coin." We know that even in classical Sanskrit literature this word had both these senses. And as in the Chhāṃdogya Upanishad the term *nishka* has been used in the sense of a "necklace" only, it cannot serve our object. But if the Upanishads are not thus of any use to us, the Brāhmaṇas which are predecessors to the Upanishads can be profitably brought into requisition in this connection. Of this class of composition the Śatapatha-Brāhmaṇa is perhaps the best known, to us, as both a well-edited text and a critical translation are available. We will therefore confine our main attention to this Brāhmaṇa. Now, in the Kāṇḍa dealing with the *Rājasūya* we have a section which treats of the *Ratha-vimochanīya* oblations. And in connection therewith we are told that behind the right hind-wheel of the cart-stand the king fastens two ROUND Śatamānas, which he has afterwards to give to the Brāhman priests as his fee for this ceremony.[1] Again, in another place the same Brāhmaṇa has the following: "Three Śatamānas are the sacrificial fee for this (offering). He presents them to the Brahman; for the Brahman neither performs (like the Adhvaryu), nor chants (like the Udgātṛi), nor recites (like the Hotṛi), and yet he is an object of respect: therefore he presents to the Brahman three

[1] V. 4. 3. 24 & 26.

Śatamānas."[1] Of course, Sāyaṇa in this and the preceding passage takes Śatamāna to denote 'a round plate,' but the case is not unlike that of Nāgojibhaṭṭa who, while commenting on the celebrated passage from the Mahābhāshya referred to in my last lecture, interprets Mauryas as idol-makers. But just as no scholar will now understand Mauryas to mean idol-manufacturers but take them to denote the Maurya princes only, no one can similarly explain the term Śatamāna in the way in which Sāyaṇa has done, but he must interpret it to denote the Śatamāna coin alone. Śatamāna may, however, have been one hundred *mānas* or *guñjā* berries in weight as explained by Sāyaṇa and accepted by Prof. Eggeling, but as it is spoken of as *vṛitta* or ROUND in shape in the first of the two instances just adduced, it must stand for coined money and not mere bullion weighing one hundred *guñjās*. I will quote two more passages from the Śatapatha-Brāhmaṇa, because in them another class of coins have been mentioned side by side with Śatamāna. The first passage is: *Suvarṇaṁ hiraṇyaṁ bhavati rūpasy=ev=āvaruddhyai Śatamānaṁ bhavati śatāyur=vai purushaḥ.*[2] The second is: *hiraṇyaṁ dakshiṇā Suvarṇam Śatamānam tasy=oktam.*[3] It will be seen that

---

[1] V. 5. 5. 16.

[2] XII. 7. 2. 13.

[3] XIII. 2. 3. 2.

8

here Suvarṇa is associated with Śatamāna, and both are called *hiraṇya* or gold. As Suvarṇa is thus distinguished from *hiraṇya*, Suvarṇa must, like Śatamāna, denote a coin, and not simply 'gold' as has been wrongly understood by Prof. Eggeling in his translation of this Brāhmaṇa. Two passages of similar import are noticeable also in the Taittirīya-Brāhmaṇa, which specify the reason why Śatamāna is given as a sacrificial fee. Here I shall cite one only, *viz. Śatamānaṁ bhavati śatāyuḥ purushaḥ śat-endriyaḥ āyushy=ev=endriye pratitishṭhati.*[1] Nay, the very same passage is traceable in the Taittirīya-Saṁhitā,[2] which, you are all aware, forms the Saṁhitā text of the Black Yajur-Veda. This means that the Śatamāna type of coin was known to the Aryan India not only in the Brāhmaṇa but also in the Saṁhitā period.

The fourteenth or concluding Kāṇḍa of the Śatapatha-Brāhmaṇa[3] gives us a story about Janaka, King of Videha. He had celebrated a sacrifice in which he bestowed huge largesses upon the Brāhmaṇs of the Kuru-Pañchāla country. A curiosity sprung up in his mind as to who was the best-read of these Brāhmaṇs. He collected a thousand kine, and we are told

---

[1] I. 7. 6. 2; I. 2. 7. 7.

[2] III. 2. 6. 3; II. 3. 11. 5.

[3] The same story is repeated in the Bṛihadāraṇyakopanishad, III. 1. 1 & ff.

that to every single horn of each cow were tied ten *pādas*, and it was proclaimed that they should be taken away by him alone who is best cognisant with *brahman*. The story further goes, as some of you here probably know, that Yājñavalkya alone had the indomitable courage of claiming them. But we are not concerned with that part of the story. What we are here concerned with is to know what those *pādas* were, ten of which were fastened to each horn of the cows. It has been suggested by Böhtlingk and Roth, and accepted by Prof. Rhys Davids [1] that the word *pāda* here denotes the fourth part of a certain gold weight but not a coin. Are we then to suppose that as the cows that were brought were one thousand in number, as each cow has two horns and as each horn carried ten Pādas, King Janaka ordered 20,000 pieces of gold to be hammered out, each again weighing just one-fourth of a certain weight,—all this just on the spur of the moment when the idea of testing the erudition of the Brāhmaṇs occurred to him [2] ? I am afraid this idea would be too ridiculous for any scholar to entertain seriously in his mind. On the other hand, Pāda is known to be the name of a coin and

---

[1] ACMC., p. 3, n. 2.

[2] Even if we suppose that to each horn of a cow was fastened gold weighing ten *pādas*, we have to assume that Janaka on the spur of the moment had 2000 pieces of gold hammered out, each conforming to that weight—which also is absurd enough.

has been referred to in one of Pāṇini's sūtras[1] and also in an inscription of the tenth century A.D.[2] Of course, it must have denoted a coin which in value was one-fourth of that coin which was the standard money, just as the modern denomination *pāvlā* or *pāvlī* which is derived from the word *pāda* denotes four annas, *i.e.* exactly one-fourth of the standard coin, *viz.* the rupee. Only if *pāda* is taken to stand for a coin, it is easy to understand that Janaka could at any moment get hold of 20,000 such coins from his treasury for being tied to the horns of the cows.

There is another class of coins referred to in the Brāhmaṇas,—I mean Kṛishṇala. Thus the Taittirīya-Brāhmaṇa has the following passage: *Kṛishṇalaṁ Kṛishṇalaṁ Vājasṛidbhyaḥ prayachchhati,*[3] *i.e.* he gives a Kṛishṇala to each racer. Kṛishṇala, we know, denotes the well-known *raktikā* or *guñjā* berry, and what Kṛishṇala here means is a coin, possibly of gold, weighing one *guñjā* berry. This receives confirmation from the fact that the Kāṭhaka-Saṁhitā makes mention of *hiraṇya* Kṛishṇala,[4] *i.e.* the gold coin Kṛishṇala. Kṛishṇala certainly continued to be known as a coin as late as the time of Manu.[5] Thus in Chapter VIII, *e.g.*, he ordains that a hired servant or workman, who, without being

---

[1] V. 1. 34. [2] EI., I, 173. 23 & 178. 11. [3] I. 3. 6. 7.
[4] XI. 4. [5] VIII. 215 & 330; IX. 84; XI. 137.

ill, out of pride fails to perform his work according to the agreement, shall be fined eight Kṛishṇalas.

It is well-known that the names of coins are also the names of metal weights. Thus not only are Nishka, Suvarṇa, etc., the names of particular classes of coins but they are also the names of the weights according to which metals are weighed. In most of the instances here adduced there can be no doubt that they are the names of coins, but in the case of a few of them some of you will, I am sure, think that the names specified may be the names of weights and not of coins. Thus in the instances of Nishkas from the Jātakas and of Kṛishṇalas which I have cited above, it may possibly be contended that it is not very satisfactorily demonstrated that they are coins, and not the weights according to which metal bullion was weighed and passed for money. Up till the advent of the British administration the practice in Burma, *e.g.*, was to carry lumps of metal as currency and chop off the required weight from the lump and tender the chip in exchange for the article wanted.[1] And it is quite possible to imagine that in the instances just referred to, gold bullion equal to one Nishka or Kṛishṇala in weight is what is meant, and not necessarily a coin of that

[1] IA., XXVI, 160.

denomination. It is, however, to be noted that in Burma there were only two denominations of weight. The smaller, according to which bullion was paid in Burma as money, was the Tickal which was almost invariably mentioned in computing money, the other and higher denomination being Viss which equalled one hundred Tickals but which was seldom used.[1] What is again noteworthy is that Tickal and Viss were employed in weighing not only money but also goods. In India, on the other hand, there were at least six denominations in the Jātaka and earlier periods, and they were used invariably to denote the weights of metal or money, but never of goods. It is again inconceivable that as six different denominations could be employed in one and the same country for paying money by weight. For, if money is to be paid by weight at all, one or two denominations are quite enough. The natural conclusion is that they all denoted not simply money weights but also denominations of coins. And even if we exclude Nishka and Kṛishṇala, I have clearly shown that all the other names could be of coins only in the instances adduced above. And it is, therefore, most unnatural to suppose that Nishka and Kṛishṇala alone denoted money weights, when Suvarṇa, Śatamāna, Māshaka and Kārshāpaṇa were all coins.

---

[1] *Ibid.*, 204-5.

But what about Nishka in the Vedic period? you are sure to interrogate me here. We see that in this period three types of gold coins were known, *viz.*, Suvarṇa, Śatamāna and Kṛishṇala. We hear about them also in the post-Vedic period, up to at least the decline and fall of the Gupta empire. But then in this later period we read about the Nishka coins also. Were they, however, known in the earlier or Vedic period, and, if so, how far earlier in this period can they be traced? This is the question that will now present itself to you. I may at once tell you that mention has been made of Nishkas both in the Brāhmaṇa and Saṁhitā sections of the Vedic literature. I suppose, some of you are acquainted with the story mentioned about Uddālaka Āruṇi in the Śatapatha[1] and Gopatha[2] Brāhmaṇas. Uddālaka Āruṇi, we are told, was driving about, as a chosen offering-priest, amongst the people of the northern country. By him a Nishka was offered to call out the timid to a disputation. Fear seized the Brāhmaṇs of the northern country, who elect Svaidāyana-Śaunaka as their champion. And a fierce wrangling arose in which, however, Svaidāyana-Śaunaka had the better of Uddālaka Āruṇi, who gave up to him the Nishka, saying, "Thou art learned,

[1] XI. 4. 1. 1 & 8.

[2] I. 3. 6.

Svaidāyana ; and, verily, gold is given unto him who knows gold."

Let us now try to find out whether there are any references to Nishka in the pre-Brāhmaṇa strata of the Vedic compositions. But here it is necessary to repeat the remark which I made sometime ago. Nishka, I then told you, is used in two senses. It signifies 'a coin' and also 'a necklace.' Many are the passages in which the word *nishka* is employed in the sense of 'a necklace,' but passages are not wanting in which the other signification of the word occurs. Thus in the Atharva-Veda, Nishka, denoting a coin, is found at least in one place. Thus we have a passage in this Veda,[1] where Kaurama, the liberal King of the Rushamas, bestows upon a Ṛishi along with other things a hundred Nishkas, which can here mean Nishka coins only, and not necklaces, because it was customary to present one necklace only to a priest and because a hundred necklaces could not be intended for the personal ornamentation of a single individual, *viz.*, the priest. Similarly, in the first Maṇḍala of the Ṛig-Veda we have a hymn in which the poet-priest Kākshīvat praises the munificence of his patron, King Bhāvayavya, thus :

शतं राज्ञो नाधमानस्य निष्कांछतमश्वान् प्रयतान्त्सद्य आदम् ।
I. 126. 2.

---

[1] XX. 127. 3.

"A hundred Nishkas from the king, beseeching, a hundred gift-steeds I at once accepted."

In regard to this passage, the authors of the "Vedic Index"[1] rightly say that "as early as the Ṛigveda traces are seen of the use of Nishkas as a sort of currency, for a singer celebrates the receipt of a hundred Nishkas and a hundred steeds: he could hardly require the Nishkas merely for purposes of personal adornment." In justice to Edward Thomas it must be said that it was he who first drew attention to this among other passages to prove the existence of metallic currency in the Ṛig-Vedic times.[2] His other passages, however, were by no means reliable, because some were misinterpreted and others were made to prove far more than was logically warranted. It is for this reason that the single passage which I have just quoted but which was first pointed out by him does not seem to have arrested the attention of scholars.

But here a question arises: what was the kind of metallic currency represented by the Nishkas in the Ṛig-Vedic times? Were they coined money or unstamped bullion currency? Let us see whether we can settle this point more precisely. Just a short while ago, I told you that as in classical, so in Vedic Sanskrit, the word *nishka* is used also in the sense of 'a

---

[1] I. 454-5.

[2] AIW., 34.

necklace.' 'Vedic Sanskrit' must, of course, include the Ṛik-Saṁhitā. From this Saṁhitā I have already quoted a verse in which *nishka* occurs in the sense of at least 'metallic currency.' If any instance of the other sense from this source is required, it is supplied by Hymn 33 of Maṇḍala II of the Ṛigveda. The line in question is :

अर्हन्विभर्षि सायकानि धन्वार्हन्निष्कं यजतं विश्वरूपम् ।

Here the god Rudra, to whom this hymn is addressed, is described as wearing a *nishka* or golden chain or necklace. But be it noted that this *nishka* is called *viśva-rūpa*. What can *viśva-rūpa* mean ? Does it signify 'omniform' ? If so, what is meant by saying that Rudra's necklace was omniform ? I am afraid this does not convey any good sense, and we must try to find out what could be the natural and proper sense of this term ? Before, however, we can hope to arrive, at any rate, at a plausible solution, we must consider the question : how could the word *nishka* come to signify both 'a currency' and a 'necklace'? Was there in the nature of things anything common which could make any one of these senses yield the other. A little reflection will tell you that this is possible only if we suppose that Nishka means not simply 'a currency' but 'a coin,' and that Nishka denoted a necklace because it consisted of Nishkas—the coins. The practice of making necklaces out of coins is prevalent almost all over India, and is by no means unknown, I am told, even in Bengal. In Mahārāshṭra, I know, the poorer classes get a goldsmith to cast gold coins in imitation of certain Byzantine originals which they call *putaḷyā*, which are afterwards strung into a necklace which also is called *putaḷyā*. If such is the case to this day in Mahārāshṭra, we can easily understand how 'a gold coin' and 'a necklace' can both be called *nishka*. The practice of fastening coins into a necklace can by no means be regarded as a feature of modern India only, but was actually in vogue in ancient times also. Thus the Jaina canonical work entitled the *Kalpa-sūtra*,[1] which describing Śrī, the goddess of beauty, whom Triśālā, mother of Mahāvīra, saw in her dream, speaks of the former as bearing *urattha-dīṇāra-mālaya*, *i.e.*, a string of Dīnāras on her breast. Now, Dīnāra, as most of you are aware, is an Indian gold coin adopted from the Roman *denarius* during the Kushana rule in the first century A.D. And here we are told that a *mālā* or necklace was made of these gold coins and adorned the breast of the goddess Śrī. The custom of stringing coins into a necklace is thus

[1] P. 44; SBE., XXII. 233. An inscription at Śrīkūrmam dated 1240 Śaka speaks of a necklace consisting of seven gold Nishka coins themselves (EI., V, 37).

not of modern origin, but was prevalent in ancient India also. It is, therefore, perfectly reasonable to say that 'a necklace' was called *nishka*, because it was made of coins called *nishkas*. *Nishka* must, therefore, be taken in the sense of 'a coin' and not merely of 'a metallic currency.' If this natural explanation is not accepted, I ask, how are you going to interpret the word *viśva-rūpa* occurring in the hymn referred to above, how can you explain satisfactorily the god Rudra's wearing a neklace that was *viśva-rūpa*. A good sense of the term *viśva-rūpa* it is possible to fix upon, only if we admit that *nishka* means a necklace, originally at any rate, consisting of Nishka coins. The *rūpa* in *viśva-rūpa* can at once be recognised to be a word technical to the old Indian science of numismatics and denoting the symbol or figure on a coin which for that reason is styled *rūpya*. The term is met with in this technical sense not only in the early Brahmanical but also in the Buddhist literature. We shall come to know more about it in the fourth lecture of this series. But suffice it to repeat here that *rūpa* signifies a symbol or figure on a coin, and this enables us at once to perceive the significance of *viśva-rūpa*. What the seer, or rather the composer of the hymn, means is that the necklace worn by the deity Rudra was composed of Nishka coins, and that just because these Nishka coins bore various *rūpas* or figures on them, the necklace was naturally *viśva-rūpa*. The earliest of coins found in India are the punch-marked coins, and we know that no less than three hundred different devices or *rūpas* have been marked on them. No wonder if the necklace of Rudra which was made of Nishka coins is described as *viśva-rūpa, i.e.*, covered with manifold *rūpas* or figures.[1] This seems to be the most natural and reasonable interpretation of the phrase *viśva-rūpa* which qualifies the term *nishka* in the sense of 'necklace.' And this is additional evidence to show that Nishkas were coined money and not merely metallic currency. In fact, unstamped metallic currency also was not unknown in the Ṛig-Vedic period, and is distinguished from the Nishkas by a distinct phraseology. Thus Maṇḍala VI contains a hymn, which is a panegyric by the Ṛishi Garga of the King Divodās, son of Śriñjaya.[2] In this hymn there is one Ṛik which enumerates the gifts bestowed by this king on the poet-priest. And among these mention is made of *daśa hiraṇya-piṇḍa* which the Ṛishi received. Now, what does *hiraṇya-piṇḍa* mean here? As these *hiraṇya-piṇḍas* have been specifically mentioned as ten, it appears that each *hiraṇya-piṇḍa* conformed to a definite recognised value. And

---

[1] This is exactly the interpretation put upon the phrase by E. Thomas, who rightly also draws our attention to *lakshaṅ-āhataṁ Dīnāra-drayam* occurring in Northern Sanskrit Buddhist texts (NO.—AIW., 35-36).

[2] VI. 47. 23.

as the word *piṇḍa* shows, it was bullion beaten into somewhat definite, *i.e.*, probably roundish, shape. The *hiraṇya-piṇḍas*, which the seer Garga received, appear, therefore, to be buttons of gold which passed as unstamped money in the Ṛig-Vedic period. Of course, there is nothing strange in both stamped and unstamped money circulating in one and the same period. Not many years ago, as you will recollect, the Ḍhābuās, which were unstamped copper coins, circulated freely in Bengal along with stamped coinage of various denominations. We need not, therefore, be surprised, if we find from the Ṛig-veda that both *hiraṇya-piṇḍas* and Nishkas, *i.e.*, unstamped and stamped money, were current at one and the same time.

Now, what is the upshot of the whole discussion? We find that not only Pāṇini's Sūtras or Buddhist Birth Stories, but all sections of the Vedic literature, contain undoubted references to the different classes of coins. Thus the coins called Kṛishṇalas, Suvarṇas, Śatamānas and Nishkas have been mentioned not only in the Brāhmaṇa but also in the Saṁhitā portions of the Vedas. The conclusion is, therefore, irresistible that the art of coining was known to India when the Vedic Aryans composed their hymns. I am aware that different scholars have propounded different theories in regard to the duration of the Vedic period, especially in regard to its initial point. Thus according to some of them the Vedic period begins from 1200, according to some from 1500 and according to some again from 2000 B.C., all however agreeing that it terminates about 500 B.C. The 'Age of the Veda' was about eleven years ago subjected to a searching and exhaustive scrutiny by Prof. Winternitz, whose views have now-a-days to be accepted. "As the result of the investigations of the last ten years," says he, "it could be said that it is *probable* that in place of 500 B.C. will have to be substituted the date 800 B.C., and it is *more probable* that the initial date falls in the third rather than in the second millennium."[1] Thus, according to Prof. Winternitz, the Vedic period in all probability extends from 2500 to 800 B.C. If this is so, coined money must be considered to be existing in India as early as the middle of the third millennium before Christ. Is it not therefore absurd to say, as Kennedy and Smith have done, that India did not know of any coined money before 400 or 700 B. C.? What is strange is that they have expressed this sweeping view even when they had E. Thomas' book before them and especially the passage from the Ṛig-veda quoted above. This, I believe, has to be attributed to the tendency of some European scholars to regard everything Indian that is good

[1] *Geschichte der Indischen Litteratur*, Pt. I, p. 258.

or original as having been adopted from the foreigners and as being of a comparatively late date. This tendency, I am afraid, even a savant like Max Müller was not able to shake off from his mind. Last year while lecturing on the ancient alphabet of India I had occasion to show how far he had exhibited it. This year it is my misfortune to point out how far he has manifested it in regard to the subject we have been considering here to-night. Max Müller emphatically maintains that "the Hindus derived their knowledge of coined money from foreign nations."[1] But then what becomes of the word Nishka which occurs in the sense of a gold coin and which was certainly known to him, he being a pre-eminent Vedic scholar? This is what he says: "Nothing seems to be more likely than that it should be derived from Kanishka, the Sanskrit name of Kanerki, as we speak of a "Sovereign," the French of a "Louis." The First syllable Ka may be taken as the usual royal prefix, particularly as Fahian calls the same king Kanika and Nika. Yet nobody would draw from this the conclusion that the Veda was written after the time of Kanishka. If Nishka be really derived from Ka-Nishka, Kanishka must have been the name or title of more ancient kings, whose money became known in India." In other words, what Max Müller means is that

[1] HASL., 331-2, and n. on 332.

there must have been foreign kings of the name or title of Kanishka before the Veda was written. And why this preposterous supposition? Because the word Nishka in the sense of 'a coin' occurs in the Ṛig-veda, and certainly the Hindus derived their knowledge of coined money from the foreign nations !! In justice to Prof. Max Müller it must be said that he does admit that "Nishka may have a very different etymology" to the one that he has proposed. But he makes this remark so incidentally and covertly as to make very little impression on the mind of the student who reads his view about the derivation of Nishka from Kanishka, and it leaves absolutely no doubt in the mind of an impartial and dispassionate scholar as to the kind of bias which has impelled Prof. Max Müller to his view. A far better judicial frame of mind has been displayed by E. Thomas, who traces the Sanskrit word *nishka* to the Semitic root *miskāl*, 'to be weighed,' but he admits that the Aryans of India "do not appear to have imported or had any knowledge of the Hebrew *shekel* of 220 grains. So that the integrity of the Indian system of weights remains altogether unaffected."[1]

I am aware that it is possible to suggest any number of etymological explanations for the word *nishka*, *e.g.*, the authors of the *Śabda-kalpa-druma* and the *Vāchaspatya* derive it from

[1] NO.—AIW., 17.

the root *nis+kai*, thus *niśchayena kāyati śobhata =iti*. But such etymologies, I am afraid, are anything but convincing. For we know that names of coins are names of weights. No derivation of the word *nishka* can therefore be acceptable to us except that from a root which means "to weigh." E. Thomas' proposal connecting it with the Semitic root signifying "to be weighed" has thus apparently something in it to commend itself to us, especially as *miscal* is also the name of a weight in Persia. But this miscal is equal to 72 grains of barley corn only, whereas a Nishka weighs 960 such grains. Whether, therefore, it is permissible to equate Nishka with Miscal is very doubtful. And even if we trace the Sanskrit word to the Semitic root, we must bear in mind that such a proposal can at best go to show that the Aryan and Semitic languages influenced each other—a conclusion that is in no way surprising. This cannot, however, be taken as evidence to show that the art of coin-making was imported into India from the Semitic country, because outside India no metallic currency is known to exist prior to 800 B.C. Besides, no Semitic word of an early period is yet known, corresponding to *nishka* in sound and denoting a weight like it. Hence Edward Thomas is right in saying that "the integrity of the Indian system of weights remains altogether unaffected."

But this is not all. The extreme antiquity of coinage is proved also from another source. The "punch-marked coins" which are the earliest of the coins hereupto discovered in India point precisely to the same conclusion. But this matter had better be reserved for the next lecture where I am treating of the Kārshāpaṇas.

LECTURE III.

KĀRSHĀPAṆA: ITS NATURE AND ANTIQUITY.

In my last lecture I discussed the question of the antiquity of coinage in India. In connection with this discussion, I had to refer principally to certain classes of coins, such as the Nishka, Śatamāna, Suvarṇa and so forth. And as these are gold coins, you may well ask now whether none but gold coinage was known in India up to the fifth century B.C. This is the first question that must suggest itself to us here. Again, if there were current in India during this early period coins of metal or metals other than gold, can we expect them also to throw some light on the question of the antiquity of coinage in India which we considered in the last lecture? This is the second question that must also occur to us. You will naturally expect me to tackle them both here. This task I will therefore impose upon myself in this lecture.

Now, the first question that I am called upon to answer, as you have just seen, is whether there were any coins known in this early period which were of metal other than gold. Even in my last lecture, if you remember rightly, I had occasion to make mention of a class of coins called Kārshāpaṇas, which is frequently referred to in the Jātaka literature, and far more frequently than the classes of gold coins, such as Nishka, Suvarṇa and so on. The Jātaka stories, at any rate such of them as contain references to coins, give us the impression that this Kārshāpaṇa was of three varities, according as it was of gold, silver and copper. Gold Kārshāpaṇa, however, appears to be seldom referred to, the common types being either silver or copper. The different divisions of this coin standard are Kārshāpaṇa, Ardha-Kārshāpaṇa, Pāda-Kārshāpaṇa, Chatur-Māshaka, Tri-Māshaka, Dvi-Māshaka, Eka-Māshaka, Ardha-Māshaka and Kākaṇikā. The values and weights of these coins will receive our full attention later on, but I have here specified the different tokens of this system in order to show how big the table for this money is. I shall now show you, in brief of course, how wide was the circulation of this money in the society depicted by the Jātaka tales. Thus the Gāmaṇī-Chaṇḍa Jātaka speaks of a king of Benares who is noted for his wisdom and impartiality. While one day he is in the judgment hall, two cases come up for consideration in which one and the same individual, namely, Gāmaṇī Chaṇḍa, is charged with having failed to return a pair of oxen which are stolen by thieves and with having caused a grievous hurt to a horse's leg. The king decides that Chaṇḍa shall pay the price of each animal to its owner, that of the pair of oxen being twenty-four and of the horse one thousand Kārshāpaṇas.[1] Of course, these must be silver Kārshāpaṇas, as copper or gold Kārshāpaṇas would be too low or too high a price to pay for those animals. Then another Jātaka gives us the story of a landed proprietor who loses his parcel of a thousand Kārshāpaṇas which falls into the river he is crossing. The parcel is, however, swallowed by a big fish which is caught by a fisherman, and is sold for seven Māshakas to the landed proprietor who is transported with joy to recover his money as his wife was dressing the fish.[2] These too must be silver Kārshāpaṇas as the seven Māshakas mentioned here as the price of the fish can be a copper token of silver money only.

Various and numerous are the details of every day life portrayed in the Jātakas where we find the Kārshāpaṇa and its small money playing an important part. Thus a professional assessor is paid eight Kārshāpaṇas as his fee,[3] and a nice plump dog is bought for one Kārshāpaṇa.[4] A

---

[1] *Jāt.* II. 305. 19; 306. 19-20.

[2] *Ibid.*, II. 424. 19-20.

[3] *Ibid.*, IV. 138. 1, 7, 16-20

[4] *Ibid.*, II. 247. 2.

decent ass is had for eight Kārshāpaṇas, and a fawn for one or two Kārshāpaṇas only.[1] A bundle of grass, again, fetches one Māshaka,[2] and for the same small coin can be had a jar of liquor.[3] A Māshaka or Ardha-Māshaka, again, is the daily wage of a coolie.[4] And a dead mouse is purchased for a single Kākaṇikā,[5] almost the lowest money piece of the day, to serve as food to a cat in a tavern, and so on and so on. In fact, whosoever reads these Jātakas carefully cannot fail to be impressed by the fact that silver Kārshāpaṇa and its smaller tokens were intimately connected not only with the commercial life but also the daily intercourse of the period to which these tales belong. Quite in keeping with this is the fact that in the early Buddhist works when any big sums of money are specified, no name of coin is adduced, that of Kārshāpaṇa being understood as is quite clear by its occasional mention.[6] Kārshāpaṇa was, therefore, looked upon as the standard coin, and the coined money stored in royal treasuries is thus described as Kārshāpaṇa.

Though in the majority of the instances in which Kārshāpaṇa is mentioned in the Jātaka

---

[1] JRAS., 1901, p. 883.

[2] *Jāt.*, III. 130. 8.

[3] *Ibid.*, I. 350. 11.

[4] *Ibid.*, III. 326. 17.

[5] *Ibid.*, I. 120. 20.

[6] *Ibid.*, IV. 378. 13-15 ; VI. 97. 1-2 etc., etc.

literature, it can refer only to the silver coin, instances are not wanting in which copper and gold Kārshāpaṇas can alone be understood to have been referred to. Thus to hire a carriage in Benares by the hour cost 8 Kārshāpaṇas. The same amount was considered to be a remuneration fit for a barber. Again, tailoring repairs well done, in a suburb of Benares, brought in money at the rate of 1,000 pieces a day.[1] Similarly, a fisherwoman is fined eight Kārshāpaṇas.[2] In these and a few more such instances it is impossible to conceive Kārshāpaṇa as being of any metal other than copper.

Gold Kārshāpaṇas also were not unknown. I shall give only one reference. The Babbu-Jātaka tells us of a merchant of the Kāśi country who, when he died, left behind a treasure of forty crores of *hirañña* or gold pieces.[3] His wife also died, but so strong was her love of money that she was re-born a mouse and dwelt over the treasure. She fell in love with a stone-cutter, so much so indeed, that she gave him at first one, but afterwards two or three, Kārshāpaṇas every day till by degrees she gave him the whole hoard. Here the treasure is stated to consist of forty crores of gold pieces which are afterwards referred to as Kārshāpaṇas by giving

---

[1] JRAS., 1901, pp. 883-4.
[2] *Jāt.*, I. 483. 21.
[3] *Ibid.*, I. 478. 7 and 16.

which the hoard is said to have been exhausted. No doubt can be entertained as to Kārshāpaṇa being here intended to denote a gold coin.

Nay, the practice of striking gold, silver and copper Kārshāpaṇas was not confined to the Jātaka period only, but seems to have continued to at least the fifth century A.D., when the celebrated commentaries on the Pāli Canon were written. The Sāmanta-pāsādikā, while explaining a verse from Pātimokkha, says about Kārshāpaṇa as follows: "*tattha Kahāpaṇo ti : suvaṇṇa-mayo vā rūpiyamayo vā pakatiko vā*, here Kārshāpaṇa is either made of gold, or that made of silver, or the ordinary one."[1] It will thus be seen that even so late as the fifth century A.D. when the commentary Sāmanta-pāsādikā was composed, Kārshāpaṇa was known to be of three kinds, *viz.*, of gold, silver and copper.

So far in regard to the Buddhist literature. It may now be asked whether the conclusions we have so far drawn on the strength of Pāli works receive any corroboration from Sanskrit literature. Those who have read Manu will be reminded of the verse: *kārshāpaṇas=tu vijñeyas-tāmrikaḥ kārshikaḥ paṇaḥ*.[2] Manu, it will be perceived, takes Kārshāpaṇa to denote a *paṇa*

[1] INO-ACMC., 8 and n. 3.
[2] VIII. 136.

or coined money which is *tāmrika, i.e.*, made of copper and is *kārshika, i.e.*, one Karsha in weight. Thus according to Manu, Kārshāpaṇa is a copper coin only, and the question arises whether there are any Sanskrit works where Kārshāpaṇa is mentioned as being also of gold and silver metals. Surely because Manu has said that Kārshāpaṇa was copper money, it does not follow that this must have been so at all times and at all places. Nārada, quoted in the *Vāchaspatya* under *karsha* regards *Kārshāpaṇa* apparently as synonymous with Paṇa and remarks that in the south Kārshāpaṇa was a silver coin. The same *Vāchaspatya*, again, under the word *Kārshāpaṇa*, gives three quotations, one from Gautama, one from Kātyāyana and one from a work called *Shaṭ-triṁśat*, and conclusively shows that Kārshāpaṇa is a synonym of Purāṇa which is known to be a silver coin only. Take also the Amarakosha which distinguishes between Kārshāpaṇa and Paṇa. Both, we are told, are *kārshika, i.e.*, one Karsha in weight,[1] but Amarasiṁha speaks of Paṇa alone as *tāmrika, i.e.*, made of copper, from which his commentators Kshīrasvāmin and Rāmāśrami infer that Kārshāpaṇa was a silver coin. If we, however, consider the statement of Amarasiṁha critically, a wider inference is permissible. All that this lexicographer implies is that Kārshā-

[1] II. 9. 88.

paṇa was not a copper coin. This may mean that it can be not only silver but also gold money. This seems to me to be the natural inference to draw in the present case. It may, however, be asked whether, as a matter of fact, there is any explicit mention of gold Kārshāpaṇa made anywhere in Sanskrit literature though this inference is permissible from the Amarakosha. I may therefore draw your attention to the gloss of the Kāśikā on Pāṇini's aphorism *jātarūpebhyaḥ parimāṇe*,[1] where two illustrations are given in verification of the *sūtra*, *viz.*, *hāṭako Nishkaḥ hāṭakaṁ Kārshāpaṇam.* Here the author of the Kāśikā speaks not only of Nishka but also of Kārshāpaṇa as being *hāṭaka*, *i.e.*, made of gold. No doubt need, therefore, be entertained as to Kārshāpaṇa being also a gold coin.

Now, what is the upshot of this whole discussion? We learn in the first place that the issue of Kārshāpaṇa was not restricted to any particular metal and that there were Kārshāpaṇas not only of copper but also of silver and gold. In favour of this conclusion is the concurrent testimony of both Brahmanical and Buddhist literature. Secondly, Kārshāpaṇa appears to have been so called, because in weight it conformed to one Karsha. We have got the authority of both Manu and Amarasiṁha in support of this position. Thirdly, one Sanskrit work

---

[1] IV. 3. 153.

entitled *Shaṭ-triṁśat* leads to the inference that the silver money called Purāṇa was also known as Kārshāpaṇa. Let us take these three points one by one and try to know about each something more. The first of these points, of course, is why there should be Kārshāpaṇa of three different metals. If Kārshāpaṇa was looked upon in those early days as the standard money, why should it have been struck in gold, silver and also copper? What could be the explanation of this strange fact? In this connection I cannot do better than quote the words of Prof. Rapson who is one of the best authorities on the pre-Muhammadan numismatics of India. In his book on Andhra and Kshatrapa coins he says: "We may gather both directly from the statement of the law-books, and more generally from the study of the coins, that in Ancient India silver and copper coinages were often independent of each other and circulated in different districts. A copper currency was not necessarily regarded as merely auxiliary to the silver currency; but a copper standard prevailed in some districts just as a silver standard prevailed in others."[1] I will verify this statement here. When Wema-Kadphises, the second Kushana ruler, introduced gold coinage in the first century A.C., it continued to be the standard money in

---

CIOBM-AKTB., Intro., clxxix.

North India for a long time and practically supplanted the silver currency of the preceding dynasties. In Mālwā, Kāṭhiāwāṛ, Gujarāt and Rājputānā, on the other hand, where the Kshatrapas exercised supremacy, the silver currency held the field. Both these gold and silver currencies were so firmly established as the standard money in these respective regions that when the Guptas succeeded these foreign dynasties in the sovereignty of India, they had to strike gold coins in the Kushana dominions in imitation of the Kushana gold coinage and silver coins in the Kshatrapa provinces after the model of the Kshatrapa silver coinage. This shows that the standard coin of one country was gold and of the other silver for a long time. On the other hand, Besnagar, the ancient Vidiśā, capital of eastern Mālwā, tells us a different tale. Here I excavated two consecutive cold seasons at a good many sites and of different periods, but from the pre-Mauryan down to the Gupta times no gold or silver coins were picked up except one solitary silver coin of Gautamīputra Yajña Śrī-Sātakarṇi, all the coins obtained being copper Kārshāpaṇas and constituting the currency of the town. This is a clear instance in my opinion of copper coinage forming the standard money. There can, therefore, be no difficulty in taking Kārshāpaṇa in any town or district to mean the standard coin whether of gold, silver or copper.

The second point we have to consider in detail is that Kārshāpaṇa was so called because it was one Karsha in weight. Manu, we have seen, says this about the copper Kārshāpaṇa only, but Amarasiṁha gives this to be the weight of all the three classes of Kārshāpaṇa. So the first question we have to answer is: what is Karsha? It is a matter of regret that the term *Karsha* has not been explained by Manu, Yājña-valkya or any law-giver. I hope you remember *e.g.*, the verse in which Manu says that Kārshā-paṇa is a copper coin weighing one Karsha. But this Karsha has not been explained by Manu in this or any verse of his Code. The term has been explained only by his commentators. Kullūka, *e.g.*, tells us that Karsha is equal to one-fourth of Pala. And as Pala is equivalent to 320 Kṛishṇalas or Ratis, we infer that Karsha was 80 Ratis in weight.

Cunningham has calculated that the average weight of Ratis is 1·83 grains. Kārshāpaṇa is thus 146·4 grains in weight. In this connection it is necessary to take the sub-divisions of the Kārshāpaṇa into consideration. For our object here is to see whether we can identify Kārshā-paṇa with any coins recovered from old sites by finding out whether the latter conform to one Karsha in weight. And this object can be best realised by seeing that not only Kārshāpaṇa but also its smaller tokens can be satisfactorily identified. A specification of these token coins occurs in two Jātakas,[1] in one passage from the Vinaya-Piṭaka,[2] and in Kauṭilya's *Artha-śāstra*.[3] An exhaustive list of the sub-divisions of the Kārshāpaṇa money, prepared from these sources, would comprise the following: Kārshāpaṇa, Half-Kārshāpaṇa, One-fourth Kārshāpaṇa, One-eighth-Kārshāpaṇa, Four-Māshaka, Three-Māshaka, Two-Māshaka, One-Māshaka, Half-Māshaka, One-Kākiṇī, and Half-Kākiṇī. Whether these smaller tokens were all of them and at any time prevalent is very doubtful. The most constant factors from amongst these seem to be Half-Kārshāpaṇa, One-fourth-Kārshāpaṇa, One-Māshaka, Half-Māshaka, One Kākiṇī and Half-Kākiṇī. These together with some of the intermediate sub-divisions appear to have formed the token money of the standard Kārshāpaṇa of any particular district or of any particular period. If, therefore, Kārshāpaṇa was one Karsha in weight and is equal to 146·4 grains according to Cunningham's calculations, in attempting to detect Kārshāpaṇa amongst the numerous types of ancient coinage in India we ought to find out not only whether there are any which conform to this weight but also those of smaller sizes which would correspond to one-half, one-fourth

---

[1] I. 340. 30; III. 448. 14-15.

[2] II. 294. 15-16.

[3] p. 84.

and so on of this weight so as to give us the smaller tokens of the Kārshāpaṇa as well.

Let us find this out, in the first place, in the case of the copper Kārshāpaṇa to which we have already confined our attention. The numismatist who has made a systematic study of the Kārshāpaṇa is Sir Alexander Cunningham, whose view would therefore naturally be worth seeking for in this matter. "The unit of the old Indian copper money," says he, "was the *pana*, weighing 80 *ratis*, or 146 grains. This was subdivided into halves, quarters, eighths and sixteenths, of all of which I possess numerous specimens."[1] Cunningham is here speaking of that class of coins called Punch-marked by authorities on Indian Numismatics, and he affirms that he was in possession of numerous specimens not only of copper Kārshāpaṇa but also of at least four of its smaller tokens. This testimony is, therefore, invaluable. But let us take another instance. I have already informed you that in the ancient Vidiśā copper Kārshāpaṇa was the standard money from slightly before the rise of the Mauryas to at least the beginning of the Gupta supremacy, *i.e.*, for upwards of 600 years. And you would naturally be curious to know whether in that ancient capital of Central India punch-marked coins of these proportionately diminishing weights were found. If you refer to my two

[1] NChr., XIII (1873), p. 202.

reports on the excavations I carried at this place,[1] you will find that the coins picked up here completely confirm Cunningham's conclusions, and also prove something more. What this 'something more' is, will be duly placed before you in the course of this lecture, but what we are here specially concerned with is that many coins were found in these excavations, corresponding in weight to 1/1, 1/2, 1/4, 1/8 and 1/16th of Karsha and thus pointing clearly to their being Kārshāpaṇa and its sub-divisions.

So far in regard to the copper Kārshāpaṇa. Let us now see what gold Kārshāpaṇa could have been. A Karsha, you have seen, is equal to 80 Ratis. Do we know of any gold coins which conform to this weight? Those who are acquainted with the metrology of the ancient coins of India will at once tell you that the gold coin called Suvarṇa has this weight, *i.e.*, weighs 80 Ratis. Take Manu, *e.g.*, who, while describing the gold standard, says: *pañcha-Kṛishṇalako Māshas=te Suvarṇas=tu shoḍaśa*,[2] *i.e.*, five Kṛishṇalakas or Ratis make one Māsha and sixteen Māshas make one Suvarṇa. Does this not make a Suvarṇa equal to 80 Ratis, the weight of the Kārshāpaṇa? Kauṭilya also gives precisely the same information in his Artha-śāstra.[3] For

[1] ASI-AR., 1913-14 p. 220 and ff.; 1914-15, p. 87.

[2] VIII. 134.

[3] p. 103.

he says that five Guñjās make one Suvarṇa-Māsha and sixteen such Māshas make one Suvarṇa or Karsha. It will be seen that according to Kauṭilya also one Suvarṇa equates 80 Guñjās, *i.e.*, 80 Ratis. But what is most important in this connection to note is that according to him another name for Suvarṇa is Karsha. Can any doubt be entertained after this as to Suvarṇa being the gold Kārshāpaṇa? Perhaps a sceptic may not be completely satisfied on this point, and may ask whether there were any subdivisions of Suvarṇa corresponding to those of Kārshāpaṇa. This is a very natural question to ask. If Kārshāpaṇa is looked upon as the standard money and if Suvarṇa is gold Kārshāpaṇa, Suvarṇa surely becomes the standard coin; and Suvarṇa cannot be admitted to be the standard coin unless it can be shown to have had its smaller tokens like those of Kārshāpaṇa. Have we got any evidence to prove this? Now, the same chapter of Kauṭilya's Artha-śāstra, that tells us that Suvarṇa is Karsha, gives us a list not only of the sub-divisions but also of the multiples of gold weights of which the unit is Suvarṇa. I will quote it here for your comparison. It runs thus: *Ardha-Māshakaḥ, Māshakaḥ, dvau, chatvāraḥ, ashṭau Māshakāḥ, (Suvarṇa ekaḥ), Suvarṇau dvau, chatvāraḥ, ashṭau Suvarṇāḥ, daśa, viṁśatiḥ, triṁśat, chatvāriṁśat, śatam=iti.* As the denominations of coins correspond to the metal weights, are we not entitled to infer from this list that Suvarṇa also had its smaller tokens similar to Kārshāpaṇa? No reasonable doubt can now be entertained as to Suvarṇa being intended as the gold Kārshāpaṇa. Unfortunately these Suvarṇas, or the gold Kārshāpaṇa, cannot be identified with any of the gold coins of ancient India that we have been able to examine or obtain.[1] Students of Indian numismatics know full well that very few gold coins have survived of the pre-Kushana period and that none of these were struck by any royal dynasties native to India. Perhaps the excavation of the sites of the Mauryan and pre-Mauryan periods may lead to the discovery of indigenous gold coins, to the existence of which we have abundant references in Vedic and post-Vedic literature as I shewed you in my last lecture.

If gold coins of genuinely Indian types have not been obtained prior to the Gupta period, silver coins at any rate have been found in abundance and of much earlier periods. Are there any from amongst them which are one Karsha in weight and may thus be regarded as representing the silver Kārshāpaṇa? This is

[1] Curiously enough, W. Theobald says: small gold coins of this class are known (JASB., 1890, p. 182). If he, however, means the gold pieces with punch marks referred to by Sir Walter Elliott on p. 54 of INO-CSI., they can hardly be designated Kārshāpaṇas. For Cunningham's view, however, see CAI., 51.

what we have now to find out. I am afraid we have to answer this question in the negative, as no coins have so far been discovered which singly weigh one Karsha. Are we therefore to suppose that there were no silver Kārshāpaṇas? How then are we to reconcile this with the fact that Purāṇas are designated Kārshāpaṇas in some of the Sanskrit works as I told you just a while ago? Purāṇa has on all hands been admitted to be a class of silver coins and known also as Dharaṇa. But Manu says that two Kṛishṇals or Ratis make one silver Māshaka and that sixteen such Māshakas make one Dharaṇa.[1] A Dharaṇa or Purāṇa is thus equal to 32 Ratis. How can a Dharaṇa by any stretch of language be called a Karsha and how can a Purāṇa be supposed to denote the silver Kārshāpaṇa? Again, the weight which Manu has specified for Purāṇa is not a figment of the imagination, because many silver coins of 32 Ratis or of approximately 58 grains have been found.[2] Why then should Purāṇa have been looked upon as representing the silver Kārshāpaṇa, when it does not weigh one Karsha? This question must, therefore, confront us here. If we now refer to the chapter from Kauṭilya's Arthaśāstra which gives an account of weights and upon which we drew just a while ago to prove that Suvarṇa was

---

[1] VIII. 135-6.

[2] NChr., XIII (1873), p. 201.

the gold Kārshāpaṇa, we find that he gives the specification of the weight of a Dharaṇa also, and what is most interesting is that this Dharaṇa is almost the same as Karsha. Thus according to Kauṭilya 88 Gaura-sarshapas or white mustard seeds equal one silver Māshaka and sixteen silver Māshakas equal one Dharaṇa. The question now is: What is the weight of a Gaura-sarshapa as compared to a Kṛishṇala or Rati. Here Manu comes to our aid as he tells us that 18 Gaura-sarshapas make 1 Kṛishṇala and 5 Kṛishṇalas 1 Māshaka. A Māshaka is thus, according to Manu, equal to 90 Gaura-sarshapas, whereas it is equal to 88 according to Kauṭilya. This difference of two white mustard seeds is so insignificant that it is a negligible quantity, especially as a mustard seed of one province cannot possibly be of exactly the same weight as that of another. Thus the Dharaṇa of Kauṭilya practically comes to 80 Ratis, the weight of a Karsha. Further it is to be noted that he specifies also the smaller tokens of this silver money, for he speaks not only of silver Paṇas but also ½ Paṇas, ¼ Paṇas and ⅛ Paṇas.[1] No rational objection can therefore be raised to Dharaṇa of Kauṭilya's description denoting the real silver Kārshāpaṇa. But here we are confronted with another question. If Dharaṇa was up till the time of Kauṭilya equal to one Karsha, why

[1] Kauṭilaya's *Arthaśāstra*, 84.

did it suffer a diminution shortly after as is clearly evinced by the actual specimens of Purāṇas we have obtained which weigh not 146 grains like a Karsha but 58 grains only? Those who have read Cunningham's book entitled "Coins of Ancient India"[1] must be familiar with his remark that India produced little or no silver. Kauṭilya,[2] on the other hand, speaks of many varieties of silver, and in no place gives us the impression that it was scarce in his time. Is it possible that shortly after Kauṭilya the sources of producing silver in India began to fail and that consequently as silver became scarce and increased in value, the Purāṇa had to be diminished in weight?

We thus see that the old Kārshāpaṇa, which is so frequently mentioned in the early Buddhist literature and Hindu law-books, can be recognised at least in the punch-marked coins from among the specimens found of the ancient coinage of India. Unfortunately no gold coins conforming to the Hindu metrological standard have been discovered of a period prior to the Gupta supremacy. But, so far as the silver or copper Kārshāpaṇa is concerned, there can be no reasonable doubt as to the punch-marked coins being among those intended. It, therefore, seems necessary now to say something more about

[1] P. 5; INO-CSI. 51 and n. 1.

[2] P. 86.

these punch-marked coins in order that you may obtain a clearer idea of the Kārshāpaṇa. If Kārshāpaṇa, as we have perceived, represents the standard money of any province, whether it be gold, silver or even copper, it stands to reason that the punch-marked coins which have been identified with them must be found all over India. Is this a fact? I have just told you that no gold coins of a Hindu dynasty have been discovered of a period anterior to the Guptas. No wonder if gold Kārshāpaṇas have not yet been identified. But what of the silver or copper Kārshāpaṇas, you may ask. I will, therefore, quote the testimony of two celebrated numismatists to show you over what wide area the punch-marked coins are found. "These silver punch-marked coins," says Cunningham, "are found all over India, from Kabul to the mouth of the Ganges, and from the Himalaya Mountains to Cape Comorin. There were 200 specimens in the South Indian collection of Mackenzie, 500 in Masson's Kabul collections, 373 in Stacy's North Indian collection, 227 in the British Museum. About 2000 have passed through my hands, and altogether I have seen between 4000 and 5000 specimens.[1]" Another numismatist, E. Thomas, makes the following remarks in regard to the range of the distribution of the Kārshāpaṇa coins. "The silver pieces of this

[1] CIA., 42.

class," says he, "the *purāṇas* of the Law-books, are found in unusual numbers, and over almost the entire length and breadth of Hindústán,—starting from the banks of the sacred Sarasvatí—to a crypt formed by nature, eighteen feet below the soil which now covers the inhumed city of ancient Behat—down the course of the Ganges to the sea, encircling the eastern and western coasts, and taking refuge even in the "Kist-vaens" of the extinct races of the Dakhin."[1] These quotations will give you an exact idea of the range of the circulation of the punch-marked coins. Of course, copper punch-marked coins also have been found, but they are comparatively few. Copper is a more perishable metal than silver. Copper coins, again, are more apt to be melted down into domestic utensils. Besides, it is quite possible that in the ancient period represented by the punch-marked coins, the standard issue was generally silver Kārshāpaṇa, occasionally copper and rarely gold Kārshāpaṇa. This may explain the proportionate paucity of the copper and gold, as compared to the silver, Kārshāpaṇas found in India.

But at this stage some of you may perhaps ask: what is meant by punch-marked coins? The term 'punch-marked,' let me tell you, is used in contradistinction to 'die-struck.' A die covers the whole or very nearly the whole of the

[1] INO.-ACMC., 53.

face of a coin, but a punch covers only a small portion of its surface so that the blank of a coin is impressed not by one but by many separate punches representing many devices and applied irregularly at various points. The face of the coin thus presents a curious appearance, consisting, as it does, of a regular net-work of symbols often overlapping. It had for a long time been thought that these symbols were the the arbitrary marks of particular shroffs and moneyers and not assignable to any particular state or locality and that they were punched into these coins haphazard by these authorities as the coins passed through their hands.[1] Dr. D. B. Spooner was the first scholar to refute this view. In November, 1906 some silver punch-marked coins were found in the Government House grounds in Peshawar. Of these only 61 could be secured, and were examined very carefully by Dr. Spooner, who contributed a paper on them to the *Annual Report* of the Archæological Survey of India. In one place in this paper he makes the following remarks—"But my tabulation of the marks occurring on the coins of the present collection tends directly to a refutation of this view. The above mentioned group of 5 symbols occurs on 20 of the 61 coins in the collection, with one symbol regularly in each corner, and one, with like regularity the

[1] COIMC., 133-4.

dharma-chakra, impressed on one edge and overlapping the nearest two. This alone would have rendered the old theory doubtful, but when it is added that in every case where the punch-mark on the reverse was decipherable it was found to be what Cunningham called the 'Taxila mark,' we have an invariable concomitance established between a particular group of 5 symbols on the obverse and a particular 'mint mark' on the reverse, which cannot conceivably be lacking in significance and which points decidedly to these coins having been the regular coinage of some one accepted central authority, and the symbols or their selection the recognised insignia of the same, *not* the private marks of individual moneyers impressed haphazard from time to time."[1] Practically the same conclusion was forced on me when I had to examine the punch-marked coins, all copper, which I picked up in my excavations at Besnagar. Here I could detect at least three classes of coins corresponding to three distinct groups of symbols found on them.[2] And it is a matter of extreme gratification that Mr. Walsh came to the same conclusion from an examination of 108 punch-marked silver coins from an earthen *ghaṛā*—found buried in the bank of the Ganges at Golakhpur in Patna City, about 15 feet below

---

[1] ASI.-AR., 1905-6, p. 153.

[2] *Ibid.*, 1913-14, p. 220 and ff.

the present surface of the ground. The interest of this find lies in the fact that the marks on the coins "occur in certain constant and regular groups on the obverse," though, of course, with a few varying additional symbols as might be expected,[1] and that these regular combinations of marks enabled Mr. Walsh to divide the coins into at least five classes. These discoveries of punch-marked coins with their provenances definitely known, give a death-blow to the theory that all symbols on them "were affixed hap-hazard by shroffs and moneyers through whose hands the coins passed," and give rise to the incontestable conclusion that they constitute "coinages" peculiar to three different provincial towns,—one belonging to Takshaśilā of North-West India, the second to Pāṭaliputra of Eastern India and the third to Vidiśā of Central India.

That different places had their constant and regular groups of symbols or mint marks peculiar to them not only can be apprehended by a critical study of these punch-marked coins, but is also attested by a passage from the *Visuddhi-magga* of Buddhaghosha to which I have already drawn the attention of scholars in my report on the excavations at Besnagar.[2] It describes how a lot of coins lying on a wooden slab would strike an inexperienced boy, a man

---

[1] JBORS., 1919, pp. 18-19.

[2] ASI.-AR., 1913-14, p. 226.

from the village, and a shroff or money-changer. The boy would notice simply that some coins were oblong, some round and some elongated in shape. The rustic would know all this, and also that coins were, like gems, worthy objects of enjoyment to mankind. The shroff, on the other hand, not only would be conversant with all this, but also would be in a position to decide, after handling the coins in a variety of ways, which of them were struck at which village, mufassil town, capital city, mountain and river bank, and also by what mint master. Is it not clear from this passage that every place which issued coinage had its own distinguishing mark or marks stamped on it, by observing which the shroff of the ancient day could at once tell from which place any particular coin came? In regard to villages and towns we have just seen that Takshaśilā, Pāṭaliputra and Vidiśā had their own individual marks on their coinage. And when a new hoard of Kārshāpaṇas is discovered, we have only to notice their provenance and such distinguishing marks in order that we might obtain knowledge of the characteristic symbols of the coins of other villages and towns. The passage from the *Visuddhimagga* also speaks of coins struck near hills or on river banks. Those who have examined the Kārshāpaṇas found at Besnagar or Eraṇ are already familiar with the sign—a zig-zag—denoting a river-bank.[1] The same sign occurs on the coins of the Western Kshatrapas along with another, which was so long wrongly supposed to stand for a *stūpa* or *chaitya* but which is now rightly perceived to represent a mountain.[2] Mr. Theobald has written an interesting paper on the significance of the symbols on punch-marked coins, and we have only to refer to the plates of his article to be convinced that there were many variations of one and the same symbol, *e.g.*, that representing a hill or a riverbank.[3] These variations of the symbols the shroffs of the early periods must have been conversant with, to enable them to tell from what different hills and river banks the coins came.

I have just alluded to Mr. Theobald's article on punch-marked coins. Therein he enumerates no less than 277 symbols occurring on them. Many more have since been discovered. But no numismatist has yet been able to give an intelligent classification of them. Mr. Theobald has no doubt made an attempt at this classification. He has thus placed these devices under six heads, namely, (1) the human figures; (2) implements, arms and works of man, including the *stūpas* or *chaityas*, bow and arrow, *etc.*;

---

[1] ASI.-AR., 1913-14 pl. LXV, Nos. 1-4 etc. ; CAI., pl. XI. Nos. 1-5.

[2] ASI-AR., 1913-14, p. 211-12.

[3] JASB., 1890, pl. VIII. nos. 46-52.

(3) animals; (4) trees, branches and fruit; (5) symbols connected with solar, planetary or Śivite worship; and (6) miscellaneous and unknown. But this classification, I am afraid, is as good as nothing, for what is gained by our being told that one group of devices is human figures; another, animals; a third, trees, and so forth? What we should like to know is the significance of the human figures, or animals such as the elephant or horse, that we find punched on the Kārshāpaṇas. Elsewhere,[1] in this connection, I have remarked that one set of symbols is certainly the seven *ratnas* or treasures, the possession of which constitutes paramount sovereignty. These have been described *e.g.*, in the *Mahā-sudassana-sutta*. They are (1) *chakra* or wheel, (2) *hastin* or elephant, (3) *aśva* or horse, (4) *maṇi* or gem, (5) *strī* or woman, (6) *grihapati* or treasurer, and (7) *pariṇāyaka* or counsellor.[2] All these symbols can be easily recognised on the Kārshāpaṇas, and their presence is quite natural and intelligible on coins which are indicative of sovereignty. In the same paper where I identified these devices I have thrown out a hint that another group of signs on these coins must consist of auspicious symbols and that some of them are certainly those met with in old cave inscriptions

---

[1] ASI-AR., 1913-14, p. 211.

[2] SBE., XI. 252 and ff.

which begin or end with them. But no scholar seems to have yet worked in this direction.

Far more interesting than the classification of these symbols is their origin ; and Mr. Theobald has done great service to the cause of ancient Indian numismatics by drawing our prominent attention to this fact. His attempt at explaining the origin of most of these marks, it is true, was not much successful, and many of his conclusions in regard to the origin of particular symbols will not commend themselves to archæologists. Nevertheless, he was the first to perceive that most of the symbols noticeable on the punch-marked coins "occur in such diverse lands as Assyria, Egypt, India and Scotland," and to trace at least fourteen of these signs which were identical with those figured on the sculptured stones of Scotland.[1] This raises an issue of paramount importance for the history of the world, and suggests a pre-historic origin of some of the marks punched on the Kārshāpaṇas. I will cite here two or three instances only to show what I mean. Take first the *svastika*, which is regarded as a symbol of auspiciousness in India to this day. We are so much accustomed to perceive this symbol in the modern homes as on the antiquities of India that we are apt to suppose that it is an auspicious symbol peculiar to this country alone.

[1] JASB., 1890, pp. 186-7.

And if it is found in Japan, China and Tibet in ancient as well as modern times, it can be explained as being imported there from India. What is, however, noteworthy is that it is found on the pre-historic antiquities of Spain, Portugal, Greece and even America. With regard to this symbol Mr. Cartailhac says as follows : "Modern Christian archæologists have obstinately contended that the Svastika was composed of four gamma, and so have called it the Croix Gammee. But the Ramayana placed it on the boat of Rama long before they had any knowledge of Greek. It is found on a number of Buddhist edifices ; the Sectarians of Vishnu placed it as a sign upon their foreheads. Burnouf says, it is the Aryan sign par excellence. It was surely a religious emblem in use in India fifteen (?) centuries before the Christian era, and thence it spread to every part. In Europe it appeared about the middle of the civilization of the *bronze age*, and we find it, pure or transformed into a cross, on a mass of objects in metal or pottery during the *first age of iron.*" It is not my object to enter into a full discussion of the origin, antiquity and dispersion of the Svastika, round which has clustered a mass of literature and for which I would refer you all to the most exhaustive treatment of it by Mr. Thomas Wilson, published in the Annual Report of the Board of Regents of the Smithsonian Institution for the year ending June 30, 1894. What, however, I wish you to note in this connection is that though in modern times the Svastika is confined to India, Tibet, China and Japan, in ancient days it was well-known all over the southern and western portion of Europe and made its appearance as early as the middle of the bronze age. The systematic study of the pre-historic archæology of India has but just begun, and has been started by this University. It would therefore be interesting to know to what early period our University colleagues are able to trace the existence of the Svastika on the prehistoric Indian antiquities.

Another symbol which is met with on the Kārshāpaṇas and later coins and to which I would invite your attention now is the sign which is supposed and wrongly supposed to represent the *stūpa* or *chaitya*. We have got at least two specimens of this symbol, on one of which a pea-cock and on the other a dog is represented as standing. If the symbol is taken to be one of a *stūpa* or *chaitya*, the presence of a pea-cock or dog on its summit is inexplicable. Cunningham was the first to suggest that it was a sign for Mount Meru,[1] and this idea was afterwards accepted by Pandit Bhagwanlal Indraji.[2] I have elsewhere expressed the

[1] NChr., XIII (1873), p. 188.
[2] BG., Vol. I, Pt. I. p. 30.

view that the symbol need not be taken to stand specifically for Mount Meru but rather for a hill in general.[1] According to this view the pea-cock or dog on its top can very well be understood to stand for the different vehicles of the different hill deities represented. Now, a seal-impression of late Minoan style has been found at Knossos which has been ascribed to circa 1500 B. C. On it figures the mountain-mother standing on the peak of her hill and flanked by guardian lions.[2] The hill on which she stands is represented as consisting of rows of semicircular curves raised in tiers exactly as the so-called *stūpa* or *chaitya* symbol does. This clearly shows that the symbol cannot possibly denote a *stūpa* or *chaitya* but rather a hill, and that this representation of the hill can be traced even outside India and to the pre-historic period, certainly earlier than 1500 B. C. to which the Knossos seal has been assigned.

Two more of the pre-historic signs occurring on the punch-marked coins. Figure 144 of Mr. Theobald's plates is described by him as "a star of eight points," and is a mark found on Kārshā-paṇas. But precisely the same sign has been observed on the megalithic pottery exhumed by Mr. Yazdani from the pre-historic cairns in the

---

[1] See note 2 on p. 101 above; JRAS., 1915, p. 412.

[2] ERE. VIII. 868; Farnell's *Cults of the Greek States*, III, 295-6 and pl. XXXIII.

Nizam's Dominions as will be seen from No. 69 of his "Diagram of marks."[1] The same symbol is noticeable also in the neolithic rock-carvings in Edakal in Malabar.[2] Again, the numismatists need not be told what is meant by the 'Ujjain symbol' Cunningham invented this designation, because the symbol frequently occurred on coins found at Ujjain The designation is, however, admitted to be defective, because the same symbol is noticeable in other parts of India. The designation is applied to an object which consists of a cross with each of its arms terminating in a ball or circle. And precisely this object is found in crosses on the Kassite cylinders in Western Asia.[3]

It would be too irksome for me to exhaust the list of the symbols on Kārshāpaṇas which have a pre-historic origin.[4] Mr. Panchanan Mitra, who is keen on the prehistoric archæology of India, is, I hear, already engaged on a systematic study of these symbols. This is just as it should be. What we have to note here is that there are not one or two but many pre-historic symbols to be found on the punch-marked coins. Mr. Theobald himself has observed not less than fourteen such, engraved on the sculptured stones

---

[1] JHAS., 1917, p. 57.

[2] IA., 1901, p. 413, No. 24.

[3] W. H Ward's *Seal Cylinders of Western Asia*, 394.

[4] Attention may also be drawn in this connection to JBORS., 1920, p. 400.

of Scotland. There was a time when Fergusson and archæologists of his kidney relegated the rude stone monuments of Great Britain and Scotland to the post-Roman period, but no archæologist of any repute now disputes its pre-historic character or assigns them to any time posterior to 1500 B. C. When therefore we find so many symbols of pre-historic origin occurring on the punch-marked coins, it is difficult to avoid the conclusion that Kārshāpaṇa coinage must have been handed down to us from pre-historic times. If any further evidence is required, it is furnished by the fact, first brought to our attention by Elliot, that these punch-marked coins "have been discovered among the ashes of the men who constructed the primitive tombs known as the *Pāṇḍukulis* (or Kistvaens) of the South, and unearthed from the ruins of buried cities in excavating the head-waters of the Ganges Canal."[1] "A large hoard of these coins," says he elsewhere, "was discovered in September, 1807, at the opening of one of the ancient tombs known by the name of *Pāṇḍukuḷis* near the village of Chavadi paleiyam in Coimbatore, thus identifying the employment of this kind of money with the aboriginal race whose places of sepulchure are scattered over every part of Southern India."[2] In regard to Pāṇḍu—kuḷis

---

[1] INO-CSI., 45.

[2] *Madras Jour. Lit. & Science*, 1858, p. 227.

or Pāṇḍu-kuṛis as they are properly called, Caldwell in his *Dravidian Grammar*[1] says as follows: "It is a remarkable circumstance that no class of Hindus know anything of the race to which these Druidical remains belonged, and that neither in Sanskrit literature nor in that of the Dravidian languages is there any tradition on the subject. The Tamil people generally call the cairns by the name of *Pāṇḍu-kuris. Kuri* means a pit or grave, and *pāṇḍu* denotes anything connected with the Pāṇḍus, to whom all over India ancient mysterious structures are attributed." It will thus be seen that quite in consonance with the indisputable fact that pre-historic signs are found on the Kārshāpaṇas is the other fact, equally indisputable, that they have been picked up also from the pre-historic cairns. I have repeatedly remarked that pre-historic archæology of India is yet in its infancy, but even taking the most unfavourable estimate of the age of these monuments, the Pāṇḍu-kuṛis, I am afraid, cannot possibly be placed later than 1500 B. C. In these circumstances the introduction of the Kārshāpaṇa coinage must be attributed to about the beginning of the second millenium before Christ. Cunningham who had far deeper insight into the age and nature of the ancient monuments of India than any of his

[1] p. 526.

successors was disposed to date these coins as early as 1000 B. C., but Smith thought this estimate to be certainly "much in excess of the truth" because his mind was obsessed with the idea that coinage began with the Lydians about 700 B. C. and that consequently there could be no coined money in India prior to that date. It is inconceivable how he stuck to this notion when the passage from Elliot regarding the find of punch-marked coins in the pre-historic Pāṇḍu-kuṛis was known to him, and has actually been quoted by him in his *Catalogue of the Coins in the Indian Museum.*[1] This is another piece of evidence, over and above that based on references to coins in the Vedic literature, to which I drew your attention in the last lecture,—I say, this is another piece of evidence which points to a much higher antiquity for the coinage of India than numismatists would fain allow. In order that I may not be misunderstood, let me make it clear to you that all that I contend is that the coinage of India must date from the pre-historic period. I do not, however, maintain thereby that the art of coinage originated in India, though the trend of evidence points to that hypothesis, no actual specimens of or even references to coins having yet been found in respect of the pre-historic age of any other country than India.

---

[1] P. 135.

Just one or two minor points connected with Kārshāpaṇa before I conclude this lecture. We have seen that Kārshāpaṇa is a coin which weighs one Karsha. We have also seen that though both Manu and Yājñavalkya speak of Kārshāpaṇa, they do not specify the weight of a Karsha, which is, however, done by their commentators and which comes to 80 Ratis. Prof. Rapson goes a step further and gives an actual table, according to which 5 Ratis or Raktikās make 1 Māsha, and 16 Māshas 1 Karsha.[1] And the same is repeated by Mrs. Rhys Davids in her "Notes on Early Economic Conditions in Northern India."[2] Whether this table is based on the authority of any Smṛiti I have not been able to find out, but certain it is, as I have already said, that neither Manu nor Yājñavalkya has given it. The same table is, however, cited by Suśruta, and, in fact, Karsha is a weight pretty familiar to the Hindu science of medicine. Thus in accordance with this table, sixteen Māshas made one Kārshāpaṇa. The commentary on the Vinaya-Piṭaka,[3] however, tells us that in the time of the king Bimbisāra five Māshakas equalled one Pāda, thus making one Kārshāpaṇa equivalent, not to sixteen, but twenty, Māshas. This receives corroboration from

---

[1] CIOBM-AKTB., Intro., clxxviii.

[2] JRAS., 1901, p 878.

[3] III. 45.

a Jātaka which, while mentioning the sub-divisions of a Kārshāpaṇa, speaks of a four-Māshaka piece as of lower value than a Pāda.[1] It is not, however, clear whether this Kārshāpaṇa, because it consisted of twenty Māshas, weighed more than 80 Ratis. It is quite possible that its weight continued to be the same, making its Māsha equal to four Ratis only, and not five.

It is worth noticing in this connection that Kauṭilya in his Arthaśāstra speaks of Paṇa, Half-Paṇa, Quarter-Paṇa and One-eighth Paṇa as silver coins, and Māshaka, Half-Māshaka, Kākaṇī and Half-Kākaṇī as copper coins.[2] This information is interesting in more than one way. For, in the first place, we see that the smallest silver coin in Kauṭilya's time was One-eighth Paṇa or Kārshāpaṇa. Secondly, the smallest copper coin in his time was Half Kākaṇī. As Kākaṇī denotes a lower denomination than Half-Māshaka, Kākaṇī could not have weighed more than one-fourth of a Māsha. Half Kākaṇī must, therefore, have weighed one-eighth of a Māsha, *i.e.*, one-eighth of five Ratis. And as one Rati is equivalent to 1·83 grains, Half-Kākaṇī must have equalled 1·14 grains at the most. Just imagine having any coin weighing only a little above one grain! Such a thing is almost inconceivable in the present age.

---

[1] Jāt., III. 448. 14-15.

[2] P. 84.

But perhaps the most complicated point we have to tackle in connection with this type of coinage is the weight of the Kārshāpaṇa and its smaller tokens. This weight problem I will place before you in a few words. Take first the weight of the copper Kārshāpaṇa. It weighs, we have seen, approximately, 146·4 grains. But, as a matter of fact, the Kārshāpaṇas of all provinces do not strictly conform to this weight; *e.g.*, among the various coins picked up by me in the Besnagar excavations the Kārshāpaṇa weighs 147·5 grains.[1] I admit it is quite possible to explain this small difference of weight by saying that the Ratikā or Guñjā seeds of the different provinces, like any other seeds, cannot be of exactly the same weight, and that this insignificant difference of 2 or 3 grains is, therefore, permissible. But take another case which, I am afraid, cannot be made explicable in this way. If the Kārshāpaṇa weighed 147·5 grains at Besnagar, the Ardha-Kārshāpaṇa must have weighed about 74 grains. But between these weights of the full and half Kārshāpaṇas, *i.e.*, between 147 and 74 grains, we have coins found at Besnagar itself which weigh 136, 114, 111·5 and 107 grains.[2] What could be the denomination of these four coins? Are we to imagine that there was also a ¾th Kārshāpaṇa? In that case it is

[1] ASI-AR., 1913-14, p. 221, No. 24; p. 224, No. 13.

[2] *Ibid.* 220-224.

true it would weigh approximately 111 grains, and among the four coins whose weights have just been mentioned there is no doubt one which weighs 111·5 grains. And there is nothing to preclude us from supposing that it represents the $\frac{3}{4}$th Kārshāpaṇa. But what about the remaining three? Their denomination cannot possibly be explained away similarly, because their weights are far removed from those of the $\frac{1}{1}$, $\frac{3}{4}$th and $\frac{1}{2}$ Kārshāpaṇas. Again, it is not the copper Kārshāpaṇas only that present this difficulty. The silver Kārshāpaṇas, or Purāṇas as they are called, give rise to the same problem. Of course, we shall not here take for our consideration any promiscuous group of Purāṇas coming from different places. But we will restrict ourselves only to those which have been discovered at one single place just as in the case of copper Kārshāpaṇas we consider only those that were found at Besnagar. Let us therefore confine ourselves, *e.g.*, to the Peshāwar hoard of Purāṇas which was reported upon by Dr. Spooner. The accepted weight of a silver Kārshāpaṇa is 58·56 grains. The weight of a half Purāṇa must therefore come to 29·28. There is really no specimen of the half Purāṇa or lower denomination in this hoard. The lowest weight to which some of these Purāṇas conform is 42·09 which is far removed from 29·28, the weight of the half Purāṇa and which cannot thus be identified with that denomination.

The other weights presented by the other Purāṇas of this hoard are 42·09, 43·92, 45·75, 47·58, 49·41, 51·24, 53·07 and 56·73. The last of these weights only, *viz.*, 56·73, comes so close to 58·56, the weight of the Purāṇa, that this difference is of no consequence, and that the coin of the Peshāwar hoard bearing that weight is apt to be regarded as a Purāṇa. We will, therefore, leave that weight out of consideration. We may also ignore the first three of these weights because they approximate to 43·92 the weight of the ¾th Purāṇa, supposing for the moment that there was such a denomination. But what about the other weights which are no less than four and which do not run close to $\frac{1}{1}$, ¾th or ½ Purāṇa? How are we to account for this mutability of weight evinced by the Kārshāpaṇa? No solution that is absolutely convincing has yet suggested itself to me. But a most probable explanation is that this reduction of weight is due to the debasement of the coin. That this reduction of weight was deliberate and systematic may be seen by a reference to the accompanying chart which sets forth the different weights to which the different Purāṇas of the Peshāwar hoard conform. In the first column have been given their weights in grains and in the second in Māshas. And it will be seen from the second column that these weights advance from 11½ to 15½ Māshas by the successive and regular rise of a ½ Māsha. The actual difference between the maximum and minimum of these weights is 14·66. And in this connection I may mention to you that I made an experiment on two different men in regard to the Kārshāpaṇas. Two Kārshāpaṇas of different weights and in different pairs were several times placed on the palms of their hands after carefully blind-folding them, and they were asked to tell which of the two coins was heavier than the other. Sometimes they were right, but sometimes they were wrong—even grievously wrong. And what amused me most was that sometimes a coin which was even 15 grains lighter was pronounced by them to be the heavier of the two. The ordinary human hand, I concluded, cannot unaided detect a difference of even 15 grains. No wonder therefore if the Purāṇas of the Peshāwar hoard were debased to the extent of 14·66 grains. The people of Gandhāra could not possibly have detected this reduction of weight by the mere touch of their hand, and the debasement of the coin, necessitated perhaps by political exigencies, could thus have been safely practised on them.

Debasement of coin, which leads to decline in weight, may be one cause of the mutability of weight noticeable in Kārshāpaṇa and its subdivisions. It must not, however, be supposed that debasement of coin is the only explanation of this phenomenon. Other causes also must have operated. I may here mention one of these most likely causes, and shall do so by selecting an instance from Mussalman numismatics. Those who have studied Mughal coinage need not be told that Aurangzeb in the earlier part of his reign issued copper Dāms of the heavy type, but that all the Dāms dating from the seventh to the forty-ninth year of his reign weighed much less.[1] This is not, however, an instance of the debasement of the currency as one is apt to suppose on first consideration. The real explanation is furnished by the *Mirāt-i-Ahmadi*, which expressly tells us that the weight of the old Dāms of Aurangzeb was 21 Māshas but that the new Dām weighed only 14 Māshas. In the Mughal period, as most of you know, there was free coinage in all metals so that any individual could bring his bullion to the mint and get it coined by bearing the cost of manufacture and paying seigniorage to government. But soon after the fifth regnal year of Aurangzeb, as the *Mirāt* informs us, the price of copper had suddenly gone up considerably, with the result that neither the state nor the merchants could find it profitable to coin copper pieces of the normal weight, which consequently lessened in quantity. This deficiency of the copper money, which was the principal circulating medium of the poorer

---

[1] JASB-NS., 1917, pp. 62-67.

classes, was a source of extreme inconvenience to them. With the sanction of the emperor the Dāms were, therefore, reduced in weight, and, as we have just seen, were reduced by no less than seven Māshas. Similar economic exigencies may have necessitated reduction of weight in the Kārshāpaṇa and its token money at different times and in different localities, such as Besnagar, to which I have referred above. And this may be another cause of the multiplicity of weight in this coinage.

I cannot conclude my lecture on the Kārshāpaṇa without taking notice of another theory which has been propounded to explain the metrological complications of this coinage. This theory was first set forth nine years ago by a French scholar called M. J. A. Decourdemanche.[1] He contends that the punch-marked coins, whether of silver or copper, constitute simply a Hindu variety of Akhæmenid Persian coinage. The latter does not differ from the former except in impression. We know that in much later times, certain Muhammadan sovereigns of India issued some coins with Hindu symbols and legends, even idolatrous in type, side by side with some coins of purely Arabic style and legend. Similarly, the Akhæmenian sovereigns struck punch-marked coins with Hindu symbols

[1] JA., XIX (1912), 117 and ff.

side by side with the Persian *sigloi*. That these coins were an Akhæminian issue he tries to prove by the fact that their weights in his opinion conform to the metric system connected with the Talent type, which first came into use either in Egypt or in the Assyro-Babylonian region and dependencies, and was the basis of the Akhæmenid coinage. To prove his point he selects punch-marked coins from Smith's *Catalogue*, and reviews their weights. Confining our attention to the silver variety, he takes, *e.g.*, five coins whose weights range between 43·6 and 46·2 grains and classes them under Triobolus of the heavy variety, whose theoretical weight is 44 grains. Some coins weighing between 40·2 and 42 grains he assigns to Tribolus of the light variety (Grs. 42). Two or three coins of 55 or 55·6 grains are called by him Tetrobolus (Grs. 56). He also traces Didrachmas of both the heavy and light variety among these punch-marked coins. But there are many silver punch-marked coins which cannot be assigned to any of the well-known sub-divisions of the Shekel (Daric). He, therefore, places them under four classes, the smallest of which weighs 26·5 grains. He takes this last class as representing $\frac{1}{8}$th of the unit, which thus comes to a Shekel of $14\frac{1}{6}$ grammes (heavy weight), and this is precisely the weight, he says, of an Egyptian Pharohic Shekel. I do not wish to take you further into the intricacies of the question, because it is unnecessary to do so.

Let us now see how far this theory solves the weight problem of the Kārshāpaṇas. I have told you that M. Decourdemanche relies upon the punch-marked coins described in Smith's *Catalogue*. But nobody knows from which provinces which of these coins came. We, however, do know the provenance of the hoard of Purāṇas upon which Dr. Spooner reported. It was undoubtedly found at Peshāwar. Nobody can dispute that Peshāwar and the surrounding region were subject to the Akhæmenian rule. But what tale do these coins tell? They reveal a gradation of weights, each gradation marked by 1·83 grains, *i.e.* exactly by half a Māsha. There are here, not one, but seven such gradations, and every one of these gradations is represented precisely by half a Māsha. I have already tried to explain why this regular progression or rather retrogression of weight is perceptible in the coins of this lot. But whatever the correct explanation may be, this much is certain that the metrical system to which these differences of weight are conformable is purely Indian, for Māsha is certainly an Indian weight. And if the punch-marked coins were really an Indian variety of the Akhæmenian coinage as maintained by M. Decourdemanche, would we have found this gradation marked, not by the Assyro-Babylonian, but by the Hindu weight, Māsha, in a hoard of coins found in a territory which certainly was once under the Akhæmenian sway? Even conceding for the moment that the punch-marked coins are Indian variety of the Akhæmenian coinage, M. Decourdemanche does not explain why the multiplicity of weight evinced by the Kārshāpaṇa coinage is reserved only for the Indian variety, and not found in Sigloi, the Persian variety, a large number of which has been discovered in the Punjāb and the frontier region. Again, one class of coins weighing about 55 grains is called Tetrobolus by him, and another weighing 46 Tribolus. A third class of coins weighing between 47·8 and 52·5 is treated as a third variety. We have thus three distinct classes of coins here. And as the difference of weight in none of these classes exceeds nine grains, I defy any ordinary human being to distinguish between these three varieties by the mere use of his hand. As they have been regarded as three different varieties, it stands to reason that they also have three different values. And if they are intended to possess different values, they must be capable of being distinguished by an ordinary individual by the mere handling. But as the difference of their weights does not go beyond nine grains, how it is possible, I ask, for an ordinary person to easily distinguish between these varieties? I am afraid, it is not possible to look upon them as so many distinct denominations of coins, and any attempt therefore to refer them to any weights of the Assyrio-Babylonian system will not carry conviction. Fourthly, M. Decourdemanche selects some coins weighing about 26·5 grains, which, he thinks, represent the smallest class; and taking that weight as equivalent to $\frac{1}{8}$th of the unit he arrives at the weight of the unit, and concludes from it that this unit is an Egyptian Pharohic Shekel. It is not, however, clear to me why he regards that 26·5 grains are the smallest weight exhibited by the silver punch-marked coins when even Smith's *Catalogue* gives a still lower weight, *viz.*, 21·5 grains. It is also not clear to me why he looks upon it as representing $\frac{1}{8}$th part only of the unit, and not any other fraction of it. These are some of the reasons for which I cannot bring myself to accept M. Decourdemanche's theory.

CHART OF PESHAWAR HOARD.[1]

No.	Weight.			No. from Dr. Spooner's Catalogue.
	Grains.	Māshas.		
(1)	56·73	15½	...	Pl. A. 14.
(2)	53·07	14½	...	Pl. A. 3.
(3)	51·24	14	...	Pl. A. 5, 8, 11, 13, 15, 17, 22, 26, 28; Pl. B. 1.
(4)	49·41	13½	...	Pl. A. 4, 9, 10, 12, 19, 20, 24, 27, 29; Pl. B. 5, 29, 31.
(5)	47·58	13	...	Pl. A. 1, 7, 18; Pl. B. 9, 11, 13, 16, 18, 21, 24, 28.
(6)	45·75	12½	...	Pl. A. 2, 6, 21, 23, 25, 30; Pl. B. 3, 4, 6, 7, 8, 12, 14, 19, 20, 22, 23, 25, 26, 27, 30.
(7)	43·92	12	...	Pl. A. 16; Pl. B. 10.
(8)	42·09	11½	...	Pl. B. 2, 15, 17.

---

[1] ASI.—AR., 1905-6, p. 160 and ff. The original article does not clearly tell us whether these punch marked coins were of silver or copper. But Dr. Spooner has kindly informed me that they are of silver.

LECTURE IV

SCIENCE OF COINAGE IN ANCIENT INDIA

Numismatics, as you are all aware, is a science which treats of coins. The study of coinage is supposed to be of comparatively recent origin, but in ancient India it seems to have been cultivated by different classes of people with different objects in view. Thus in the Mahāvagga of the Southern Buddhist Canon we are told a story about a boy named Upāli.[1] There was in Rājagṛiha a group of seventeen boys, friends of each other and all under twenty years of age. The most pre-eminent of them was Upāli. Now, Upāli's father and mother thought: "How will Upāli after our death live a life of ease and without pain? If he learns *Lekha*, his fingers will become sore. If he learns *Gaṇanā*, his breast will become diseased. If, again, he learns *Rūpa*, his eyes will suffer. Now here are the Śākyaputra Śramaṇas who live a commodious life; they have good meals and lie down on beds protected from the wind. If Upāli," thought his father and mother, "could

[1] SBE., XIII. 201 and ff.

be ordained with the Śākyaputra Śramaṇas, he would after our death live a life of ease and without pain." It is not necessary to tell you the whole story. Suffice it to say that Upāli and his companions got themselves ordained one day, and in the night at dawn set up such a fearful howl for rice-milk and hard and soft food that Buddha is aroused from his sleep who promptly ascertains the cause of that noise and forbids in future to confer ordination on any person under twenty years of age. But what do we learn from the story? We have here seventeen boys on this side of twenty and not far removed from it, and the parents of one of them, *viz.* Upāli, seriously thinking of introducing him to an avocation which will enable him to live a life of ease and comfort. Evidently, therefore, *Lekha*, *Gaṇanā* and *Rūpa* must be so interpreted as to denote each a profession. It is no use, therefore, taking them to be merely the "three R's" as Bühler[1] and Rhys Davids have done. *Lekha* thus cannot here signify learning to write A, B, C, but rather 'the art of writing,' which constitutes the profession of a Lekhaka. This 'art of writing' included not only the niceties of diction and style but also the different forms of correspondence, as will be seen from Chapter X of the *Adhyaksha-prachāra* of Kauṭilya's Arthaśāstra, which in its concluding

---

[1] IS., III. 13.

verse tells us that there were not one but many treatises on the subject. The word *gaṇanā* for similar reasons cannot mean 'arithmetic' but rather 'accounts' corresponding to *gāṇanikya* of Kauṭilya. Even in later times this word had this meaning, and we thus find the term *Gaṇanā-pati* used by Kalhaṇa in his *Rāja-taraṅgiṇī*[1] and understood correctly by Sir Aurel Stein to denote 'Head of Account Office.' Study of *Gaṇanā* would thus make a candidate qualified to hold a post in the Akshapaṭala Department. The third word *Rūpa* is taken by Rhys Davids to mean 'money-changing' and by Bühler 'commercial and agricultural arithmetic.' Even this meaning is not quite correct, though these scholars are here not far wide of the mark, because they were careful enough to avail themselves of Buddhaghosha's commentary which says that he who learns the *Rūpa-sutta* must "turn over and over many Kārshāpaṇas and look at them." But anybody who has read Kauṭilya's Arthaśāstra knows that the word *rūpa* has been employed in this work to denote "coins." Thus in Chapter XII of the *Adhyaksha-prachāra* Kauṭilya speaks of *rūpya-rūpa* and *tāmra-rūpa*, which cannot but signify 'silver and copper coins' respectively. He also specifies an officer called *Rūpadarśaka*, whose duty was to examine the coins in actual

[1] V. 26.

circulation or received as revenue into the royal treasury. No doubt can, therefore, be entertained as to the term *rūpa* meaning 'a coin.' so that when the parents of Upāli once thought of training him in *Rūpa* for his profession, especially as he was not far removed from twenty, we can only understand that the boy was intended to study the science of coinage only, to fit him to be either a Rūpadarśaka or Sauvarṇika.

To what class Upāli belonged is not clear. But certain it is that he was neither a Brāhmaṇ nor a Kshatriya. We shall, therefore, now take an instance in which a Kshatriya is said to have studied *Rūpa*. Some of you will perhaps have guessed that I intend here referring to Khāravela, the ruler of Kaliṅga. In a cave called Hāthigumphā in the Udayagiri hill, three miles from Bhubaneswar, in the Puri District of Orissa, we have got a long inscription of this king, describing the different events of the different years of his reign. In line 2 of this epigraph we are told that for the first fifteen years of his age he was a *kumāra* and played children's games. From his sixteenth to his twenty-fourth year he was a Yuvarāja or heir-apparent, and during this period he is represented to have mastered *Lekha*, *Rūpa*, *Gaṇanā* and *Vyavahāra*.[1] The first three of these terms are

[1] JBORS., 1917, pp. 453 and 481.

exactly identical with those employed in the story narrated of Upāli, and must therefore bear each the same signification. It is true that neither *Lekha*, nor *Rūpa*, nor *Gaṇanā* can be a source of living to a prince. Nevertheless, it cannot be denied that they must form a most essential factor of his education. A prince must learn *Lekha*, *i.e.* not merely writing A, B, C, but rather the artful style of writing and the different forms of royal writ. Similarly, in order that he may effect minimum of expenditure and maximum of receipts, he must be an adept in the science of *Gaṇanā*. The science of *Rūpa* also he cannot afford to ignore, for on his knowledge of it depend the tiding over of a financial crisis and the various methods of augmenting his revenue.

It will thus be seen that *Rūpa* had been recognised to be a science of coinage in ancient India. That it was looked upon as a science is clear, I think, from the fact that Buddhaghosha, while commenting on the passage from the Mahāvagga adverted to above, speaks of it as *Rūpa-sutta* which can only mean a set of rules concerning coins, in other words, the science of coinage. It was studied as we have seen by an ordinary individual for pursuing a profession to enable him to turn either a Rūpadarśaka, Lakṣhaṇādhyaksha or Sauvarṇika. It was also a subject of serious study to a prince to make him fit for administration. *Rūpa* must, therefore, have been a science of coins which dealt with this subject, not only from the minter's and assayer's but also from the economist's and administrator's point of view.

Unfortunately for India, this Rūpa-sūtra or science of coinage has been lost to us. The very word *rūpa* in the sense of 'coins' is scarcely met with in Sanskrit and Prakrit literature from the beginning of the Christian era onwards. The term *rūpa* we now find replaced by *mudrā*, but we do not hear of any *mudrā-sūtra* or *mudrā-śāstra*, bearing this signification. This is an exceedingly grievous and irreparable loss to the historian, and the only course left to us now is to recover as much knowledge of this science as we can from a critical study of the actual coins of ancient India that have been so far picked up and also from stray references to the art of coinage preserved to us in the works of literature. It is not impossible to reconstruct, in part at least, a science and history of numismatics from the sources just alluded to. To this task I will therefore set myself in this and the next lecture.

I have already informed you that *rūpa* in the sense of 'coins' occurs in Kauṭilya's Arthaśāstra. I have referred to the words *rūpya-rūpa* and *tāmra-rūpa* which he employs and which can mean 'silver and copper coins' only. I have also referred to an officer called Rūpadarśaka by him whose duty was to examine coins whether in circulation or brought to the royal treasury. To the period when Kauṭilya lived has been assigned Kātyāyana the grammarian, who composed *vārtikas* on Pāṇini's *sūtras*. In his gloss on Pāṇini's *sūtra* I. 4.52, Kātyāyana gives a *vārtika* which Patañjali illustrates by: *paśyati Rūpatarkaḥ Kārshāpaṇaṁ darśayati Rūpatarkaṁ Kārshāpaṇam.* What exact bearing this example has upon the *sūtra* and the *vārtika* need not trouble us here. It is sufficient for our purpose if we understand the meaning of the words as they stand. They mean: "a Rūpatarka examines a Kārshāpaṇa, and (he) causes a Rūpatarka to examine a Kārshāpaṇa." Here the inspection of a coin called Kārshāpaṇa is associated with a Rūpatarka, and it is difficult to avoid the conclusion that the Rūpatarka of Patañjali is identical with the Rūpadarśaka of Kauṭilya. It will thus be seen that *rūpa* in the sense of a 'coin' was known not only in the time of Kauṭilya but also Patañjali. If the term *rūpa* signifying a 'coin' was current from the time of Kauṭilya to that of Patañjali, there is nothing strange in our finding the word used in the early Pāli scriptures of the Buddhists. One instance will suffice here. About a century after the death of Buddha, the venerable Yaśa, while touring, once came to Vesāli and was staying with the

Vajjian Bhikshus. One Uposatha day he was shocked to find the Bhikshus filling a copper-pot with water and placing it in the midst of the Saṁgha and saying to their lay-disciples: 'Give sirs, to the Saṁgha One, One-half, or One-fourth, Kārshāpaṇa, or a Māshaka-rūpa.'[1] Here the word *rūpa* obviously signifies 'a coin,' and the Māshaka-rūpa denotes a token coin of Kārshāpaṇa known as Māshaka, as I have shown in the last lecture. This import of the term *rūpa* survived to a very late period, though it was by no means much in vogue after the beginning of the Christian era.[2] Thus the word *rūpa* or rather *rūpaka* occurs in the Rāja-taraṅgiṇī,[3] where in the sixth book a Brāhmaṇ is represented as telling to King Yaśaskara a pitiful tale of the loss of his money. This money, we are told, consisted of one hundred *suvarṇa-rūpakas*, which Sir Aurel Stein has rightly translated by 'gold coins,' and the same hoard is thrice referred to again as *rūpakas*. Rāja-taraṅgiṇī is not the only work of the late period which contains the word *rūpaka* with the meaning of 'a coin.' It has been traced, *e.g.*, also in the Kathāsarit-sāgara,[4] where in one place the Dīnāras have been referred to as *svarṇa-rūpakas*, or gold coins.

---

[1] VP., II. 294; SBE., XX. 387.

[2] See also *Kāśikā* on Pāṇini, V. 1. 48-9, where *Rūpaka* is used in the sense of a 'coin.'

[3] VI. 45, 52, 60 and 66.

[4] 78. 11 and 13.

It will thus be seen that one of the senses of the word *rūpa* or *rūpaka* is 'coin' and that the Rūpa-sūtra, mentioned by Buddhaghosha, can very well signify "the science or art of coinage." But it is worthy of note that side by side with *rūpa* we have another term, *viz.* *rūpya* which also is employed in the sense of 'a coin.' This word must have been current even prior to Pāṇini as he teaches its formation in the well-known Sūtra *rūpād=āhata-praśaṁsayor=yap.*[1] The Sūtra says that the affiix *ya* comes in the sense of *matup*, after the word *rūpa*, when *āhata* (stamping) or *praśaṁsā* (praise) is denoted. Thus *rūpyo* (*gauḥ*) means *praśastaṁ rūpam=asy=āsti*, *i.e.* one with a praiseworthy form; in other words, it means a good-looking bull. This is an instance of the word *rūpya* when *praśaṁsā* or praise is intended. But then what is the instance of this word where *āhata* or stamping is denoted? Unfortunately for us this Sūtra is not commented upon by Kātyāyana or Patañjali, and the Kāśikākāra is the first grammarian whose gloss is available to us. Nevertheless even this gloss is of great importance. And in regard to the use of the term *rūpya* where the sense of *āhata*, *i.e.* of 'hammering or stamping' is intended, we are given the following instances: *āhataṁ rūpam asya rūpyo Dīnāraḥ rūpyaḥ Kedāraḥ rūpyaṁ Kārshāpaṇaṁ.* The word *rūpya* thus denotes

---

[1] V. 2.120.

something on which a *rūpa* or figure is stamped. And what objects are these on which figures are stamped? The Kāśikākāra tells us that they are Dīnāra, Kedāra and Kārshāpaṇa. Very few of you perhaps know what Kedāra means. But most of you certainly know that Dīnāra and Kārshāpaṇa are names of coins. The term *rūpya* thus denotes coins, and coins only, when the sense of *āhata* is understood. If any doubt remains on this point, it will I hope be removed by a consideration of what the Amarakosha says regarding this word. This lexicon refers to *rūpya* in two places. In one, *rūpya* is called 'stamped gold or silver,'[1] and one commentary on it styled *Ṭīkāsarvasva* gives a detailed explanation by saying that *rūpya* denotes "Dīnāras etc. struck with a hammer so as to cause the *rūpa* or figure of a man to rise on it both on the obverse and the reverse."[2] The Amarakosha[3] also speaks of Rūpyādhyaksha who is explained to be no other than Naishkika. Kshīrasvāmin, who is looked upon as the most erudite commentator on this lexicon, says that *rūpya* in *Rūpyādhyaksha* denotes Dīnāra and other coins, and *Naishkika* a *ṭankapati* or mint-master. In other words, Rūpyādhyaksha is already a mint-master according to Amara. If Rūpyādhyaksha can

---

[1] *Amara*, II. 9.92.

[2] (TSS. No. LI), p. 231.

[3] II. 8.7.

signify a mint-master, no doubt can be possibly entertained as to the term *rūpya* denoting 'a coin.' The only question that may be legitimately asked here is whether this word was known to Pāli literature as it has been mentioned by Pāṇini on the one hand and Amara on the other. Unless the word can be shown to be occurring in the Pāli literature also, it may be contended and with some force, no doubt, that it could not have been current among the people in general. I will, therefore, cite one instance from this literature. There are two verses in the Pātimokkha which relate to monetary transactions. I will translate them here as follows: "(v. 18) If again a mendicant should receive *jātarūpa* or gold and *rajata* or silver, or get some one to receive it for him, or allow it to be put in deposit for him, it is a fault requiring restitution. (v. 19) If again a mendicant should engage in any transactions of coined money, it is a fault requiring restitution." The expression with which we are chiefly concerned here is *rūpiya-saṁvohāra, i.e. rūpya-saṁvyavahāra,* which I have rendered by "transactions of *rūpya* or coined money." This translation alone can be correct, for the monetary transactions referred to in the first of these verses are distinguished from those in the second, and if the former refer only to gold and silver bullion in the first verse, the word *rūpya* in the second verse cannot possibly mean 'silver bullion' again, but must denote 'coined money' whether of gold, silver or any other metal.

We thus see that *rūpa* and *rūpya* both mean coined money, and that both the words were prevalent at the same time. If *rūpya* signified any metal piece on which a *rūpa* was stamped, the question naturally arises: how is it that both these words of which one is a derivative of the other were being used in one and the same period? Has this strange phenomenon any foundation in fact? In other words, were there any pieces of coined money which were so shaped that they were the *rūpas, i.e.* figures or representations of any real objects, and was there again another kind of coined money in circulation which consisted of metallic pieces, not shaped like, but impressed with, these *rūpas*? If for any unknown reasons evidence of this nature is not forthcoming from India, is it supplied by the pre-historic or historic archæology of countries outside India? This is the question that now confronts us. In fact, this was the question that confronted me when I was engaged upon the study of numismatics for these lectures. As Mr. Panchanan Mitra is the Lecturer of this University on pre-historic archæology, naturally I turned to him for discussion of this subject as I did in the question of the origin of the

Brāhmī alphabet on which I lectured to you last year; and he was able to draw my attention to the researches of Prof. Ridgeway who has familiarised the antiquarian world by bringing the anthropological method to bear upon the interpretation of ancient history, especially, of Greece. Prof. Ridgeway's main contention is that while mythological and religious subjects do occur on Greek coins, it can be shown that certain coins, even in historical times, were regarded as the representations of the objects of barter of more primitive times.[1] I will cite one typical instance. It is well known that the tunny fish continually passes in vast shoals through the sea of Marmora from the Black Sea to the Mediterranean. This fish must therefore have formed the staple commodity of the communities that lived in those regions, and we know that the article which forms such a staple commodity forms money in the age of barter. Now, the city of Olbia, which lay on the north shore of the Black Sea was a Milesian colony, and was the Greek emporium in that region. There are bronze coins of this city which are shaped like fishes and inscribed with θγ which is taken to be the abbreviation of θύγγος, *i.e.* tunny, the fish. When we recall the Chinese bronze cowries, the Burmese silver shells, the silver fish hooks of the Indian

[1] Ridgeway's *Origin of Currency and Weight Standards*, 315-7.

Ocean, etc., we are constrained to believe that in these coins of Olbia, shaped like fish, we have a distinct proof of the influence on the Greek mind of the same principle which has impelled other peoples to imitate in metal the older object of barter which a metal currency is replacing. Take now the case of the city of Cyzicus, situated on the coast of Asia Minor. Cyzicus, too, like Olbania, was a Greek autonomous city and depended for its wealth on its fisheries and trade. It too had its coins, but of electrum and not of bronze like those of Olbania. The coins of Cyzicus, again, were connected with the tunny fish. They, however, bore a representation of this fish on them and were not shaped like it as was the case with the coins of Olbania. The inhabitants of Olbania, though they were originally a Greek colony, were largely intermixed with the surrounding barbarians, and may, therefore, have felt some difficulty in replacing their barter unit by a round piece of metal bearing merely the imprint of a fish, while the pure-blooded Greek of Cyzicus had no hesitation in mentally bridging the gulf between a real fish and a piece of metal merely stamped with a fish, and did not require the intermediate step of first shaping his metal unit into the form of a tunny. Here then we have two Greek cities of one and the same period, *viz.* Olbania whose bronze coins were shaped like a tunny fish, and Cyzicus, whose electrum coins merely bore the imprint of the fish, the tunny fish being in both cases their medium of barter which their metallic currency afterwards superseded. The coins of Olbania were thus the *rūpas*, *i.e.* coins which were the figures or images of the fish, whereas those of Cyzicus were the *rūpyas*, *i.e.* coins on which the *rūpa*, *i.e.* figure or representation, of a fish was impressed. A similar thing must have happened in the prehistoric or proto-historic period of India : that is to say, while the system of barter was being replaced by metallic currency, in some parts of India the metal unit must have been shaped like the article of barter, and in some parts the former merely contained the imprint of the latter. There could thus be some coins which were *rūpas*, and some, *rūpyas*. Unless some such explanation is adduced, it is impossible to understand how both the words *rūpa* and *rūpya* in the sense of 'coined money' were current side by side.

The instance which I have adduced to bring home to you the exact difference between *rūpa* and *rūpya* classes of coinage is from the Greek numismatics of the proto-historic period. But you will perhaps be curious to know whether there is any evidence to show that there was any kind of *rūpa* coins ever prevalent in India even though no specimens are available now. I may therefore draw your attention to a type of coinage called Kapardaka-Purāṇa, which is not unfrequently mentioned in the copper-plate grants of the Sena dynasty. Thus the Naihāṭī grant of Ballāla Sena records the grant of a village, Vāllahiṭṭhā, whose annual income is stated to be 500 Kapardaka-Purāṇas.[1] Or take the Tarpaṇḍīghī plates of Lakshmaṇa Sena which registers the grant of a piece of land which is specified to have annually yielded a sum of 150 Kapardaka-Purāṇas.[2] In other Sena grants also this coin has been mentioned.[3] But what can a Kapardaka-Purāṇa be? Can it denote a Purāṇa which is equal to one Kapardaka or cowrie in value? This is impossible, because a Purāṇa must contain 32 Ratis of silver, which can never be equal to one cowrie in value. The only other sense possible is that Kapardaka-Purāṇa is a Purāṇa which is shaped like a Kapardaka or cowrie. If the Chinese had metallic cowries[4] and the Egyptians gold representations of them,[5] there is nothing strange at all in Bengal having Kapardaka-Purāṇas or silver cowries as metallic currency at least during the Sena period. Kapardaka-Purāṇa of the

---

[1] EI., XIV. 161. 46.

[2] *Ibid*, XII. 9. 37-8.

[3] R. D. Banerji's *Prāchīna Mudrā*, 14-5.

[4] J. W. Jackson's *Shells as Evidence of the Migrations of Early Culture*, 178 and 205; JRAS., 1888, p. 428 and ff.

[5] G. E. Smith's *The Evolution of the Dragon*, 222.

Sena inscription must thus represent a Rūpa class of coinage.

Let us now see of what different substances the coins were made in ancient India. In this connection, allow me to draw your attention to a passage from the commentary on the Vinaya-Piṭaka which I had occasion to refer to partly in my last lecture. Of course, it is scarcely necessary to repeat that the commentary was composed by the celebrated Buddhaghosha in the 5th century A. D. The passage is concerned with Kārshāpaṇa and its sub-division, the Māshaka. We are told that the Kārshāpaṇa may be composed of gold or silver or may be the ordinary one, *i.e.* made of copper. The Māshaka, we are further informed, may be of three different varieties.[1] One variety is that composed of copper, iron or some other metal Another variety is that made of *sāra* wood, the outside of the bamboo, or palmyra leaf, each of which has been turned into the Māshaka coin by a *rūpa* or figure being cut into it. The third variety consists of lac or gum on which a *rūpa* or figure has been caused to rise up and which has thus become a Māshaka. And Buddhaghosha winds up by saying that there are other kinds of money which are current in the different parts of the country but which have not been referred to

[1] NO.—AIW., 42 n.; INO.—ACMC., 8.

by him. They are of bone or skin or the fruits or seeds of trees, and may be with or without a *rūpa* raised on it. This, in short, is the substance of the passage, and serves a rich pabulum to the numismatist. The very first conclusion that a careful consideration of this passage will suggest to you is the wide range of the meaning assigned to the term 'coin,' and it is with this conclusion really that we are concerned here. What do you generally understand by a coin? I will take here the definition which has been given by V. A. Smith, and which is the one generally accepted. Coins, according to him, denote "metallic pieces of definite weight authenticated as currency by marks recognised as a guarantee of value."[1] Thus in all classes coins to be coins must be metallic pieces. But at least two classes of Māshaka specified by Buddhaghosha were certainly not of metal. The Māshakas, which were made of wood, bamboo or palmleaf or which consisted of lac or gum, cannot possibly be described as metallic pieces. Māshakas, however, were a class of coins. And as the two kinds of money just referred to have been designated as Māshakas, they must be regarded as coins. And, as a matter of fact, we know that they bore *rūpas* on them, which certainly were "marks recognised as a guarantee of value." No doubt can possibly

[1] IGI., II. 135.

be entertained as to these two classes of money being looked upon as coins by the people though they were not made of metal. Evidently they understood the term 'coin' in a much wider sense than we do now.

We shall now first take the metals of which coins were composed. The passage from Buddhaghosha's commentary, we have just seen, speaks of four such metals, *viz.* gold, silver, copper and iron. Coins of gold, silver and copper belonging to the pre-Muhammadan period have been found in numbers. No ancient coin of iron, however, has yet been found; at any rate, none is yet known to me. And even in the modern period I have not been able to trace more than one reference to it. Mention of an iron coin has been made by W. Elliot in connection with the old coinage of the Travancore State.[1] It must not be supposed that these are the only metals of which coins were made in ancient India. Lead, nickel and mixed metals like potin and billon were also brought into requisition. Thus the *Nidāna-kathā* prefixed to the Jātakas speaks of the *sīsa-Kāhāpana* or lead Kārshāpaṇas. And, as a matter of fact, lead coins are found issued shortly before and after the beginning of the Christian era and both in north and south India. The use of lead for the first time

[1] INO.—CSI., 137.

occurs in the coinages of Strato, Azes and Rañjubula who ruled over north India and before or about the commencement of the Christian era. Lead coinage was issued also by the Andhrabhṛitya dynasty, and is found exclusively in the Andhradeśa, the home of the race, in the Anantpur and Cuddapah Districts and in the region of the Coromandel Coast. Lead currency is found exclusively also in the Chitaldrug and the Kārwār District but issued by the Mahārathis and the Kadambas.[1] And it is associated with potin coinage in the Kolhāpur province struck by Viḷivāyakura and his successors. Lead coinage seems to have been temporarily introduced apparently by the Mahākshatrapa Rudrasena III in Mālwā and during the period when silver coins are not found.

As regards the use of nickel for coinage, Cunningham was the first to trace it in the money of the Indo-Grecian kings.[2] While once he was carefully examining the coins of Euthydemus, Agathokles and Pantaleon which had been described as silver, a suspicion crossed his mind, and he sent some specimens of them to Dr. Walter Flight for analysis. The coins were found to contain a considerable amount of nickel and in proportions differing

---

[1] CICBM.—AKTB., Intro., cxlv and ff. and clxxxii and ff.

[2] NChr. XIII (1873), 188 and ff.

but little from those of the nickel pieces of Belgium. Dr. Flight's analysis produced a sensation, because "nickel was first shown to be a metal by Cronstedt in 1751." Whether nickel was used for coinage in India before the time of these Indo-Grecian princes is not certain. But Cunningham draws our attention to the statement of Quintus Curtius that "near the junction of the Five Punjab Rivers, Alexander received from the Oxydracæ and Malli, a present of 100 talents of 'white iron' (*ferri candidi*)." This 'white iron' can be either tin or nickel. But tin was a soft metal and therefore unsuitable for coinage. Besides, it was well-known to the Greeks who could not have therefore described it as 'white iron.' Nickel, on the other hand, thinks Cunningham, is hard and magnetic as well as white, and as it was not known to the Greeks, they could justly call it 'white iron.' Thus in his opinion nickel was employed for the purposes of currency by the Indian tribes Kshaudrakas and Mālavas in the time of Alexander and consequently certainly prior to that of the Indo-Grecian dynasties.

The other mixed metals that were used for minting coins in ancient India are potin and billon. The term 'potin' has been invented by the numismatists[1] to denote an alloy which is

[1] Babelon, *Traité des monnaies greeques et romaines*, I. 371.

composed of yellow and red copper, lead, tin and some dross. And according to the varying proportions of its first two ingredients they look sometimes like bronze and sometimes like lead. Again, billon is to silver what potin is to bronze. I have already made reference to the fact that potin coinage was struck along with lead coinage by Viḷivāyakura and his successors in the district round about Kolhāpur. Potin coinage was issued also by the Andhrabhṛitya kings, but exclusively in the Chāndā District of the Central Provinces. The Kshatrapa dynasty founded by Chashṭana had also its potin coinage, but curiously enough it was struck by the Mahākshatrapas of the family, was confined to Mālwā, and was discontinued soon after A.D. 236.

We have already seen on the authority of Buddhaghosha that there were some coins, *viz.* the Māshakas, which were made of wood, bamboo, palm-leaf, and even lac, and impressed with a *rūpa*. He further tells us that there were also pieces of bone and leather or fruits and seeds of trees which passed for money and which were with or without a *rūpa*. As all these substances are of a perishable nature, it is not surprising that these varieties of money have not been preserved. Prof. Rhys Davids has, however, drawn our attention to a lacquer medal which was in the possession of Col. Pearse, and says that it may represent the lacquer Māshaka coin referred to by Buddhaghosha.[1] Which of these substances, and up to what periods, were employed for the purposes of money is a subject which has not yet been properly investigated. It is nevertheless a subject on which investigation not only is possible but also will be of an interesting nature. I may here give one instance. Among the multifarious objects out of which, as Buddhaghosha informs us, money was made, is *chamma*, *i.e.* leather. As leather is a perishable substance, no specimens of leather-money which were in circulation for any length of time can be expected to be found anywhere now, and, as a matter of fact, none has yet been found. Again, *primâ facie*, leather is a substance which seems so unfit for the purposes of coinage that having not yet discovered any single leather-coin,[2] one begins to suspect whether Buddhaghosha, after all, was not drawing upon his imagination. But we have good evidence to show that there was some kind of leather-money actually prevalent in Mahārāshṭra in the thirteenth century A.D., *i.e.* full eight hundred years even after Buddhaghosha. Some of you may have

---

[1] INO.—AOMO., 8.

[2] In this connection I may refer to a story occurring in *Khulasat-ut-Tawārikh* to which Mr. Zafar Hasan drew my attention. A certain water-carrier saved the life of Humayun who therefore seated the former on his throne for half a day, and during this short period the water-carrier is reported to have issued coins out of his leather bag. But none of these coins has yet been found.

heard of the earliest poet-saint of Mahārāshṭra called Jñānadeva. He composed his Marāṭhī commentary on the Bhagavadgītā in Śaka 1212 =1290 A.D., when the Yādava king Rāmachandra was ruling over the Dekkan. In his commentary on Chapter IX of the Divine Lay there are two *Ovī* verses which are worth considering and which I translate here as literally as possible. "If but the letters of the royal order are on a scrap of leather, through that very leather are all commodities obtainable (v. 453). Even gold and silver have no value without those letters. The royal order is the principal thing. If a single leather piece of that kind is obtained, all things become purchasable (v. 454)." I have thus placed a literal translation before you. And I have done so purposely, because I myself do not know what exact conclusion to draw from it. Of course, we have here a clear reference to leather-money, but whether it is leather-coins or currency notes I confess I am unable to determine.

We shall now turn to another subject connected with ancient Indian numismatics, *viz.*, the shape and the technic manufacture of coins. I hope you remember the passage from the *Visuddhimagga* to which I drew your attention in my last lecture. Buddhaghosha therein describes the Kārshāpaṇas lying on the wooden board of a Hairaṇyika or goldsmith, and incidentally speaks of their various shapes. They are *chitra-vichitra* or 'of irregular form,' *dīrgha* or elongated, *chaturasra* or rectangular, and *parimaṇḍala* or circular. And, as a matter of fact, we do find coins of all these forms, especially among the Kārshāpaṇas. Thus there are some punch-marked coins which are unsymmetrical in form, that is to say, which have practically no regular shape. These most probably are referred to by the term *chitra-vichitra*. Coins of this class alone can be called 'rude and ugly' or 'singularly crude and ugly' as no doubt some archæologists have designated the 'punch-marked' coins in general. The elongated or the rectangular form of the coins calls for no comments, because numerous specimens of these have been known. The *parimaṇḍala* or round form of the coins, however, requires to be considered here, because the Indian coins are believed to be typically oblong, and not round. This view is held by almost all numismatists, including even Cunningham.[1] But it is a mistake to suppose that there were no coins circular in form among the Kārshāpaṇas, which are now accepted to be the most ancient and indigenous money of India. If you look to Nos. 7, 11 and 12 on Plate XIX in Smith's *Catalogue*, you will at once see that they are round Kārshāpaṇas and also that they scarcely deserve to be

[1] NChr., XIII. 207 and 213; CAI., 52-3.

called 'rude and ugly.' Even on the sculpture of Bharhut which represents the famous story of the purchase of the garden of Prince Jeta by the merchant Anāthapiṇḍika covering the ground surface of the garden with coins, *all* the pieces represented are not square as assumed by Cunningham.[1] There are some in this sculpture which are distinctly round, and the wonder of it is how this escaped his notice. It is hinted by some numismatists that the Hindus for the first time adopted the round form for their coins from the Indo-Bactrian Greeks. But this is a mere surmise, for which no evidence has been adduced, or rather which is opposed to all evidence. For in the first place what about the coins bearing on them the legends *Vaṭasvaka* and *Kādasa*? Cunningham attributes them to a date "anterior to the Greek conquest of Alexander." Bühler, however, holds that it is perhaps safer to say "anterior to the Greek conquest of Demetrius."[2] Anyhow these coins are admitted to be of a time prior to the rise of the Indo-Bactrian power. But are they not round in shape? Nay, the Indians knew of round coins long long anterior to the Greek conquest of Demetrius or Alexander. In my second lecture, I hope you remember, I had occasion to refer to a passage from

---

[1] CAI., 53.

[2] IS., III. 48.

the Śatapatha-Brāhmaṇa, which speaks of the practice of a king fastening two Śatamāna coins to a back wheel of his chariot in a particular portion of the Rājasūya ceremony. And it is worthy of note that these Śatamānas are expressly stated to be *vṛitta* or round in form. It is not thus possible to assert that the circular form of the coins was first suggested to the Hindus when the Indo-Bactrian Greeks came in contact with them.

Now, a few words about the manufacture of coins or rather the mode of evolution in the technique of the Indian indigenous coinage. The Indians seem to have begun with "a hammered sheet, which was then cut into strips, and subdivided into lengths of approximately the desired weight, which was adjusted by clipping the corners when necessary."[1] Nobody can examine any lot of punch-marked coins without perceiving that this was the mode of manufacture. There was, however, one small difference in regard to punching. In a few cases punches were applied to the surface of the hammered sheet before it was cut into strips. This is clear from the fact that sometimes some of the symbols punched are not to be seen in full on these coins. In a good many cases, however, the strips seem to have been cut out first and then punched. On all

[1] CCIM., 134.

the coins belonging to this initial stage we find symbols impressed on them irregularly and by separate punches. The first stage of progress is marked where a group of these symbols forms a distinct type, and is impressed not each by a separate punch but is struck by a single die, which, however, covers not the whole, but about two-thirds, of the piece. But the reverse face here remains blank.[1] "The next advance may be traced in the adaptation of the anvil to the first crude idea of a reverse, in a sunk-die or catch of small dimensions cut into the anvil itself."[2] The third stage is thus represented by coins where the obverse die covers the whole face but the reverse die is smaller than the blank.[3] The last stage is of course indicated by the full double-die system where the whole face is covered by a die whether on the obverse or the reverse. "The final adoption of the 'double-die' system," says V. A. Smith, "was undoubtedly due to Greek and Roman example."[4] What Smith's remark comes to is that the Indians were, of course, capable of introducing improvement into and thus developing the technic manufacture of coins before the advent of the Greeks, but their last step,

---

[1] IC., II. § 46.
[2] NO.—AIW., 54.
[3] NChr., XIII. 207.
[4] IGl., II. 137.

although it was the natural culmination of their gradual advance in the indigenous numismatic art, they could effect only when the Macedonians came to teach them!!!

"Another mechanical means—specially favoured by the aptitude of the home workmen in that direction—consisted in the casting of coins. We can only follow the general progress of this art by the merits of the devices employed, which gradually improve in treatment and finish."[1]

We now come to the consideration of the administrative aspect of the science of ancient Indian coinage. And the first question that arises here for our consideration is: who exercised the prerogative of coinage. Of course, so far as the historic times go, this prerogative pertained to the Sovereign, whether it was Sovereign One or Sovereign Number. That most of the old coins were issued by rulers foreign or indigenous to India is too well-known to require any demonstration. And I had more than one occasion to tell you that coins were issued not only by individual rulers but also by Gaṇas or Oligarchies, Naigamas or Autonomous Cities, and Janapadas or Provincial Democracies. Coinage thus was the special privilege of the state in ancient India. I am aware that instances of what may

[1] NO.—AIW., 55.

be called 'Temple coinage' are by no means unknown, and I may draw your attention in this connection to a paper contributed by Mr. Robert Sewell to the *Indian Antiquary*, 1903. In this paper he describes coins which were struck at the principal temples in southern India. It is true that they were not connected with any regular state issues, but there is every reason to suppose that they were nevertheless struck by, or, at any rate, with the sanction of, the state. And, in fact, this is admitted by Mr. Sewell himself. For in regard to certain temple coins struck in the Pudukottah State we are distinctly told by him that four such are given by the Rajah of Pudukottah to each recipient of his rice-dole, distributed in honour of the festival of Dusserah. It, therefore, stands uncontroverted that the prerogative of coinage belongs to the state. This does not, however, mean that the state did not sometimes permit private individuals or firms to coin money, whether of the higher or lower denominations. Of course, in modern times we have instances of both these kinds. Thus about Central India at the beginning of the nineteenth century Sir John Malcolm tells us that the work of coining was vested in no particular body or individuals, and that any banker or merchant sufficiently conversant in the business, had merely to apply to Government, presenting a trifling acknowledgment and engaging to produce coin of the regulated standard, and pay the proper fees on its being assayed and permitted to pass current. This must refer to coins of higher value.[1] Similarly, as V. A. Smith informs us, "to this day the people of Bihar and Gorakhpur prefer the unauthorised 'dumpy pice' made at private mints in Nepal to the lawful copper coinage of the British Government."[2] This, of course, must refer to the token coinage issued by private agencies to supply the gaps which State issues leave unfilled and thus facilitate small transactions. It will thus be seen that coins are known in modern times to have been occasionally struck by private agencies which are of both higher and lower denominations. And so the question arises whether private coinage of this description was at all known to ancient India. I confess no conclusive evidence has yet been adduced in support of this position. I am aware that some coins found in the Punjab with the word *negamā* on the obverse have been looked upon by Bühler and others as token money issued by local mercantile guilds. But I have elsewhere shown that the word *negamā*, though it can mean 'traders' or 'merchants,' can never denote 'a guild' but must stand for the *naigamāḥ*

---

[1] Malcolm's *Central India*, II. 80-1.

[2] IGI., II. 138.

of the Smṛitis in the sense of 'townsmen' collectively, *i.e.* a city-state. I am also not unaware that punch-marked coinage is regarded by V. A. Smith as "a private coinage issued by guilds and silversmiths with the permission of the ruling powers."[1] Smith is here echoing the opinion of Prof. Rapson but with some difference. He holds that the obverse punches were impressed by different moneyers through whose hands the pieces passed. According to Prof. Rapson, if I have understood him correctly, all the obverse punches may in some cases be ascribed to individual merchants.[2] Smith's view involves the assumption that the obverse punches were invariably impressed in a haphazard fashion. This view has been shown utterly untenable by Dr. Spooner, as I told you in my last lecture. When the obverse devices are in most cases found to occur in constant and regular groups, no sane scholar can subscribe to the view that they were affixed haphazard by shroffs and moneyers. But the question that presents itself to us here is whether these different groups of symbols were the characteristic marks of different merchants as contended by Prof. Rapson or of different localities as maintained by Dr. Spooner. Of course, such of these groups as contain the river or the hill symbol, *e.g.*, can scarcely be

---

[1] CCIM., 133.

[2] JRAS., 1895, p. 874.

thought to be the distinguishing devices of individual merchants, but must be taken to be the peculiar marks of localities, as I showed in my last lecture. There can therefore be no doubt as to some of these groups being the special marks of special towns and villages to which the coins bearing those groups must be assigned. Nevertheless, some of the groups may have belonged to individual merchants as is held by Prof. Rapson. This is not at all unlikely, though it cannot be definitely proved.

The next point that must engage our attention is: who were the officials connected with coinage. The only source of our information on this point is Kauṭilya's Arthaśāstra. Unfortunately it does not supply us with much information. Nevertheless, what little we can glean from it is valuable. The first official that may be mentioned is Lakshaṇādhyaksha, or Rūpyādhyaksha as he is called in the Amarakosha. He is obviously Superintendent of Mint. Kauṭilya speaks of him but once. "The Superintendent of Mint," says he, "shall manufacture silver coins (*rūpya-rūpa*), such as Paṇa, Half Paṇa, Quarter Paṇa and One-eighth Paṇa consisting of four parts of copper and one-sixteenth part (*māsha*) of any one of the metals *tīkshṇa*, *trapu*, *sīsa* and *añjana*, (and shall manufacture) copper coins (*tāmra-rūpa*) such as Māshaka, Half Māshaka, Kākaṇī and Half Kākaṇī, consisting of four parts of alloy." In my last lecture I showed you what light this passage throws on Kārshāpaṇa and its token money. What we are concerned with here is the proportion in which the metal of the coin is mixed with its alloy. In the case of copper coins the alloy forms one-fourth, and in the case of silver, five-sixteenth, part of the whole piece. Many years ago, Sir Alexander Cunningham had assays made of no less than 113 silver Kārshāpaṇas, and he found that the amount of silver in them varied from 75·2 to 86·2 per cent. This is perhaps the reason why Smith remarks about these coins that "the metal is usually impure silver, containing about 20 per cent of alloy." But certainly they contain far more silver than was the case in the time of Kauṭilya who allows as much as 31·25 per cent of alloy.

It is a pity that Kauṭilya gives us no information about the subordinates who served under Lakshaṇādhyaksha or about the process in which coins were manufactured in his time. The second officer he mentions in connection with coins is Rūpadarśaka. "Rūpadarśaka," says he, "shall establish the circulation of coined money (*paṇa-yātrā*), whether relating to commercial transactions or admissible into the treasury. (The premia levied on coins) shall be (from the manufacturer) 8 per cent known as *rūpika*, (from the seller and purchaser) 5 per cent as *vyājī*, (from the appraiser) one-eighth Paṇa per cent as *Pārīkshika*, and a fine of 25 Paṇas from (persons) other than the manufacturer, the seller and the purchaser, or the appraiser." Now, what does this passage tell us? It appears that there was regular trade carried on in coined money in Kauṭilya's time. In the first place, it seems that there was a system of free coinage, that is to say, any private individual could bring any quantity of bullion to the mint for being coined on his own account. For this he had to pay the premium of 8 per cent called Rūpika. Secondly, there was a regular sale and purchase of coins going on, for which both the parties had to pay 5 per cent on their profit to the state. Thirdly, there appears to have been a class of men called Parīkshitṛi, or Pārakhs in modern parlance, who remained in business locality and to whom the people brought, for appraising, coins coming from all quarters in the course of commerce. These appraisers must certainly have derived some profit, though perhaps not a huge one as compared with the first two classes of dealers, and had therefore to pay only one-eighth per cent called Pārīkshika. It is possible to conceive that in these monetary transactions there was occasionally transgression of law, and such offenders were punished with a fine of twenty-five Paṇas. All these transactions, it will be seen, relate to the commercial sphere, *i.e.* to *vyavahārika-paṇa-yātrā*, as Kauṭilya calls it. Rūpadarśaka had to regulate this traffic in coins, and also collect whatever was due to the state on that account. But the Rūpadarśaka was not connected with coin transactions going on in the commercial circles only. He had also to supervise *Kośa-praveśya-paṇa-yātrā*, that is to say, the coined money to be entered into the royal treasury. In another place, Kauṭilya tells us that the officer called Sannidhātṛi shall receive into the treasury only such *hiraṇya* or gold coins as have been declared to be pure by Rūpadarśaka and destroy those that are not genuine. What this exactly means we do not know. But certainly money must pour into royal treasury in a variety of ways, such as taxes, tribute and so forth. There is therefore every chance of counterfeit coins being also smuggled along with good money. And it seems that it was the duty of the Rūpadarśaka to see that none but genuine coins were deposited in the treasury.

It is not to be expected that such a big officer as Rūpadarśaka could personally examine all coins and detect those that were counterfeit. He must have had a number of officials under him, and this must have been the duty of one of them. The name of this subordinate official has nowhere been mentioned by Kauṭilya, but, from the passage of Buddhaghosa's *Visuddhi-magga* to which I have more than once drawn your attention, it appears that he could be no other than Hairaṇyika or Sauvarṇika as he has been termed in Kauṭilya's Arthaśāstra. One of his duties, as I have mentioned to you in my last lecture, was to find out at what village, town, hill or river and by what mint-master any particular coin was struck. Another function of his was to detect what coin was genuine, what counterfeit, and what partly genuine and partly counterfeit. And we are told that he performed these duties by observing the coins, by handling them, by sounding, smelling and even licking them. It is not quite clear why the Hairaṇyikas had to use their senses of smell and taste. At any rate none of the shroffs of the modern day who are their successors are known to make use of these senses. Is it possible that they had to use them to distinguish between wood, bamboo, palm-leaf, seed and similar coins which must have been in existence as I have shown to you already on the authority of Buddhaghosha?

We have just seen that it was the duty of the Rūpadarśaka and his Assistants such as Hairaṇyika to distinguish between genuine and counterfeit coins. For the facilitation of monetary transactions it was essential that coins of fixed weight or value should be in circulation. No wonder if we find Kauṭilya laying down that the manufacturer of counterfeit coins shall be banished, as also those who deal in such coins or try to lower their quality by mixing them with alloys. Those who have read Yājñavalkya need not be told how this law-giver prescribes the highest fine for those who falsify a *nāṇaka* or coin or knowingly use such a one. This is just as it should be. But although it was necessary for a state to take such drastic steps for the prevention of the manufacture of counterfeit coins or of the tampering with the currency, sometimes the Government was itself compelled to take just that sort of action which it wanted to suppress in others. Of course, I am not here referring to the cases in which in consequence of economic circumstances there is an increase in the price of a particular metal out of which coins are made and in which the state is therefore forced to reduce the usual fixed weight of any denomination of its coins. I hope you remember what I said in my last lecture about a species of copper coinage prevalent in Aurangzeb's time. Owing to the enhancement of the price of copper, the weight of these copper Dāms, as I told you, had to be curtailed by as much as seven Māshas. A similar cause may have operated, as I also then told you, in reducing the weight of copper Kārshāpaṇa and its tokens at some periods in the ancient town of Vidiśā and may thus explain in one way the discrepancy of weight in that class of coinage. Such also must have been the case in the time of Kauṭilya. I told you a short while ago that Kauṭilya's Arthaśāstra allowed as much as 31·25 p.c. of alloy in silver coins, whereas the silver Kārshāpaṇas assayed by Cunningham contained only 20 p.c. of it. This means that during the period when Kauṭilya lived, silver had become so expensive that economic exigencics necessitated a higher percentage of alloy being mixed with it in order that the original standard of value might be maintained. This admixture of a larger percentage of alloy is perfectly intelligible and justifiable, and this can hardly be called debasement of coinage. But I am not here referring to such cases, but rather to those cases where deterioration or sophistication of the currency was deliberate and was necessitated by the exhausted condition of the state treasury or by the disturbed political condition of the country. Thus if Kauṭilya prescribes that silver coins shall comprise 31·25 p.c. of alloy, one can only infer that in his time silver had augmented in value. But if Kauṭilya is credited or rather discredited, as in some Buddhist works, with having converted (by recoining) each Kārshāpaṇa into eight for the purpose of raising resources and thus having amassed 80 crores of Kārshāpaṇas,[1] the motive could have been purely political and the step surreptitiously taken to avoid any confidence of the people being shaken in the supposed purity and value of the

[1] HASL., 289; NO.—AIW., 41.

currency in circulation. How Kauṭilya recoined one Kārshāpaṇa into eight we do not know, but it would be interesting to find out what were some of the methods practised in ancient days. This is not impossible to find out, because we have only to separate true coins from those which are of a suspicious character, and subject the latter to a rigorous examination. Such a thing has not yet been systematically attempted; nor is it my object to do so here, because there are not yet enough materials for it. My object here is to draw your attention to certain old Kārshāpaṇas which have been admitted to be adulterated in order that some young numismatist here may in the near future devote his special attention to this subject. One of the commonest methods of debasing coinage is undoubtedly by increasing the admixture of alloy. But in what quantity this alloy was mixed in different periods and in different parts of the country it is not possible to know unless coins of various types are actually subjected to a chemical analysis. The tabulation of the results of such an analysis must enable us to arrive at important conclusions. Now that the Archæological Chemist has been given by Government to the Archæological Department, let us hope that before long such a tabulation will be made ready for the study of those interested in Indian numismatics. Another method of adulterating the currency is that well described by Theobald. "Some coins," says he, "are formed of a copper blank thickly covered with silver, before receiving the impression of the punches, and this contemporary (if not time-honoured) sophistication of the currency is found to occur subsequently in various Indian coinages, in the Græco-Bactrian of the Punjab, the Hindu kings of Kabul, and later still in various Muhammadan dynasties of the peninsula. The plating is extremely well executed and of the most durable character, covering the edge of the coin as well as its surface. I was for sometime at a loss to know by what means this was effected, so long ago as 500 B.C. perhaps, but I am told that a bright copper 'blank' dipped into melted silver would become coated with that metal, and this I have little doubt was the plan followed. By this means a number of copper 'blanks' thrown into a ladle of melted silver and well stirred about, would all come out ready for the impression of the die or punch and it is possible that 'blanks' thus surreptitiously prepared may have been introduced into the royal mint, and there struck with genuine dies, and the coins thus prepared substituted for an equal number of genuine pieces."[1] This is indeed a very cunning mode of multiplying currency in times of political stress when treasury is depleted but more money urgently required. This again is a

[1] JASB., 1890, 182.

method which cannot arouse suspicion, for plated coins, until thoroughly worn, are, certainly in look and finish, exact equals of those composed entirely of silver. Specimens of plated coinage are by no means unfrequent. They were detected, *e.g.*, by Mr. E. H. C. Walsh in a find of punch-marked coins in Patna City. He has found many coins in this hoard which were however sophisticated by a different method. He says that when these coins were found thickly coated with verdigris deposit which accounted for as much as 13 per cent. of the weight of the coins after they were cleaned. "The reason for this large amount of copper," says he, "is due to the faet that, apart from any proportion of alloy in the coin, several of the coins have been debased by the addition of molten copper to the original silver coin, presumably to make up for weight. That this was subsequently added is shown by the fact that it remains over the punch marks."[1]

It is thus quite conceivable that the Rūpasūtra of ancient India treated of various subjects connected with coinage, such as (1) the metals and other substances out of which coins were made, (2) their shape and technique, (3) the different devices on them and how to find out therefrom at what different places they were manufactured, (4) the running of a mint, (5) the

[1] JBORS., 1919, 16-17.

various officers connected not only with the manufacture but also with the regulation of traffic in coined money, (6) the methods of differentiating genuine from counterfeit coins, and, (7) above all, the modes of multiplying currency mostly, I am afraid, by cunning sophistication. It is also quite conceivable that this Rūpa-sūtra can be an object of serious study not only to a private individual for his avocation but also to a prince for the purposes of administration.

LECTURE V

HISTORY OF COINAGE IN ANCIENT INDIA.

In this lecture I propose to deal, briefly of course, with the history of coinage in ancient India. I am afraid, I shall have here to go over some of the ground which I have traversed in my previous lectures. The earliest period to which the use of coinage can be traced is that which saw the rise and development of the Vedic literature. As Professor Winternitz has told us, this period commences in all probability with 2500 B.C. I hope you remember his views on this point which I quoted in my second lecture when I was discussing the 'Antiquity of Coinage.' In my third lecture, as you will remember, I had to treat of the Kārshāpaṇa coinage, specimens of which are reported to have been picked up in the excavations of the Pāṇḍu-kuṛis or megaliths of India with which the southern part especially is studded. The date of these megaliths unfortunately has not yet been definitely established; and although it is possible that some of them were anterior to the Aryan immigration into India, it is on the whole safe to assign them to 1500 B.C., *i.e.* later than the beginning of the Vedic period. It will thus be seen that the remotest antiquity to which the use of coins can be traced is, after all, the beginning of the Vedic period.

The earliest composition of the Vedic period is, as you all know, represented by the hymns of the Ṛig-Veda. And in my second lecture I had occasion to tell you that in the Ṛigvedic period itself there were two types of metallic currency, prevalent side by side. One of them was known as *hiraṇya-piṇḍa* or buttons of gold, and the other *nishka* which were actually gold coins. If at the beginning of the Vedic period stamped money was current side by side with unstamped money, it is clear that the metallic currency of India must have had an earlier origin, *i.e.* an origin earlier than the time of even the Ṛig-Veda. And if such is the case with the metallic coinage of this country, the age when any kind of currency first originated in India must be pushed back still earlier. Hence before we actually begin the history of coinage in ancient India, it seems desirable to say a few words, or rather to make a few guesses, in regard to the condition of currency that may have prevailed in this country before the advent of the Aryans. I can quite imagine at this stage some doubt crossing the mind of most of you here as to how I could even surmise the state of currency in pre-Vedic India. But what Professor Ridgeway has done in regard to the pre-historic or proto-historic currency of Greece can also be attempted on a modest scale in regard to India provided we follow his method which is typically the anthropological method. It is possible to study the various kinds of currency in use amongst the savage tribes of various stages of civilisation and compare them to the similar ones that were prevalent in India, whether in the proto-historic or even the historic period. If you, for instance, concentrate your attention on the Sūtras of Pāṇini, especially those which are comprised in the sections called *tena krītaṁ* and *tad-arhati*, it cannot fail to make a very interesting economic history of India. You will find that not only coins of different types and metals were current in Pāṇini's time, but that many transactions used to take place with the help of many media of exchange. Three instances will suffice here. The first is Sūtra V. 1. 27, which shows that objects could sometimes be purchased with *vasana* or "pieces of cloth of definite value," a practice which is still followed in some parts of India, notably Rājputānā. Nay, if you turn to Sūtra V. 1. 19, you will find that the people of India in Pāṇini's time sometimes employed even a *go-puchchha* or bovine tail as a circulating medium. A similar practice, I am told, is prevalent to this day in Nepāl, where the tail of a yak, a species of ox, which is used as *chaurie*, is exchanged for other commodities. But whether this yak-tail is actually denoted by Pāṇini's *go-puchchha* is more than doubtful, because the proper Sanskrit word for the former is *chamara* which occurs also in early works such as the Mahābhārata. And *go-puchchha*, I am afraid, has to be understood in the primary sense of a cow's tail, howsoever polluting and revolting such a custom may now appear to us. There are, again, at least three Sūtras in Pāṇini's *Ashṭādhyāyī*, which speak of *kaṁsa*, *śūrpa* and *khārī* in connection with purchase of commodities. But as these are clearly measures of capacity, the only inference possible is that such commodities were bought by means of these measures and most probably with grains which were the staple food of a province. To this day the custom of purchasing things with food-stuff, such as rice grains, is not unknown in India, especially in rural regions. Now just see what these Sūtras teach us in regard to the different classes of articles that were used for currency purposes. Of course, coins were known in Pāṇini's time, and, as some of their names again are also of metal weights, we can imagine that metals by weight were also used as currency as they no doubt were in Burma till the middle of the nineteenth century. But if it is supposed that because some sort of metallic currency or another was prevalent in Pāṇini's time, there were no media of exchange in use such as we find in more or less uncivilised tribes of the modern day, I am afraid this supposition cannot be regarded as well-founded. For these media of exchange not only were prevalent in the time of Pāṇini, but have survived to this day as I have just told you. And it is not very difficult to imagine what different measures of value came into existence in ancient India with what different stages of civilisation.

Now, the earliest stage of civilisation is taken to be the Hunting Stage. No form of currency belonging to this stage, such as skins of hunting animals, is known to us from any composition of the Vedic period, or from any other source. As the Hunting Stage passes to the Pastoral, and animals are domesticated, the animal itself, not its skin, becomes the unit of value. The most common of such animals in India is the cow which is found mentioned in the Ṛig-Veda. Thus there is a hymn in this Veda[1] where Indra, *i.e.* his image, is offered as a fetish for ten cows, and another,[2] where Indra is considered to be so invaluable that not a hundred, a thousand, or even a myriad of cows is thought to be a proper price. As the Pastoral develops into the

[1] IV, 24. 10. [2] VIII, 1. 5.

Agricultural Stage, a number of agricultural products come to be used as currency, the most remarkable instance of which is corn, the staple food of a province. It is in this Agricultural Stage that commerce is found to develop itself, and a greater number of objects are found capable of being used as measures of value, such as garments, coverlets, and goat-skins which were so employed in the time of the Atharvaveda.[1] Mineral products also such as cowries come to be used first as ornaments and then as currency. You will thus see that traces of the various circulating media of these various stages of civilisation are clearly found even in the Saṁhitā portion of the Vedas and that they must have survived down to the Vedic epoch from previous stages of civilisation in India as some of them have no doubt survived to this day. But it is only when metals become substances for money that a fairly high degree of civilisation is supposed to have been reached. And clear references even to this form of money are contained in all parts of Vedic literature, not excluding the Ṛig-Veda which is the earliest.

The employment of metals as money material was thus known to India about the beginning of the Vedic period, *i.e.* circa 2500 B.C. as I have told you. It is impossible however to

---

[1] IV. 7. 6.

determine the exact order of their appearance in this capacity. The various kinds of metals that were used for currency in ancient India I had occasion to mention in my last lecture, as you will remember. They are gold, silver, copper, lead, even nickel, and such mixed metals as potin and bilion. Although it is not possible, as I have just stated, to find out in what order they came to be employed for the purposes of coining, I cannot help saying that gold appears to be the earliest metal that was so used. For all references to coins in the Saṁhitā portion of the Vedic literature relate to gold currency only.

When metals first came to be used as a money substance, they must have been weighed in scales and then given away. The people evidently must have carried small scales and weighed with them to effect purchases as they no doubt did in Burma till even the middle of the nineteenth century. What these weights were in ancient India most of you, I believe, know. Different standards were prevalent for different metals, one for the weighing of gold, another of silver, and a third of copper. What is, however, noteworthy is that these standards start all alike from Rati or Raktikā which denotes the red seed, as Kṛishṇala the black seed, of the Guñjā creeper. Already in the Saṁhitā period, the word Kṛishṇala is known to the Hindus, as it occurs in the Taittirīya[1] and other Saṁhitās. But there were other natural seeds also which were connected with the metric system, the most important of which is Māsha, *Phaseolus Radiatus*, a pulse seed marked with black and grey spots. But there were two kinds of Māshas. One was used in weighing gold and equalled 5 Kṛishṇalas, and the other was employed for weighing silver and was equivalent to 2 Kṛishṇalas only. It is possible to conceive that there were different kinds of Māshas varying in weight and size, due to the varied influences of soil and climate, and that one kind was employed to weigh gold and the other to weigh silver. Raktikā or Kṛishṇala, however, was the real unit, for even the gold and silver Māshas we find reduced to the Guñjā seeds. The old Hindu mind, accustomed to fine analysis, was not content with stopping at Raktikā or Rati, the metric unit though it was, but has gone further and divided it into a number of submultiples—which is more or less fanciful. Thus a Raktikā, we are told, is in weight equivalent to 1296 Trasareṇus, a Trasareṇu being the smallest mote we observe in a sunbeam passing through a lattice. And between the Raktikā and the Trasareṇu have been mentioned a number of natural seeds, namely, barley-corn, white mustard-seed, black

---

[1] ii. 3. 2. 1 etc.

mustard-seed and poppy-seed. These are mere theoretical state ments, and, in actual practice, the Raktikā was the universal standard. Appended to this lecture will be found two Tables, one showing the multiples, and the other, sub-multiples, of the Raktikā, together with their weights in English grains.

Let me, at this stage, remind you of what I told you in my last lecture about the *Rūpa* and *Rūpya* classes of coinage, which must have come into existence soon after, if not about the time when, metal came to be employed as money material. The words *rūpa* and *rūpya* both signify coins. As *rūpa* means 'a symbol, a figure,' *rūpya* must denote an object bearing this symbol or figure. One can, therefore, easily understand how Rūpya can stand for coins, because coins are objects on which symbols or figures are impressed or imprinted. But why should Rūpa denote coins at all? Were there any coins which were actual figures so that they could with propriety be called Rūpa? I hope you remember the instance which I gave from Greek archæology. There were two Greek colonies, where the tunny fish was the measure of value. And when metallic currency replaced this staple commodity as medium of exchange, while one colony had for its coins metallic pieces imprinted with the figure of this fish, the other had these not imprinted but actually shaped like the tunny fish. The former certainly represented the Rūpya and the latter the Rūpa class of coinage. This example is from Greek Archæology of the proto-historic epoch, but I also gave another example from India though of the historic period. Copper plate charters of the Sena Dynasty of Bengal constantly speak of Kapardaka-Purāṇa. But what does this phrase mean ? It cannot possibly mean a Purāṇa which was equal to one Kapardaka or cowrie. For a Purāṇa is a silver coin weighing about 58 grains, and no silver coin, weighing so much as 58 grains, can possibly be equivalent to one shell cowrie in value. The only possible sense here is that Kapardaka-Purāṇa is a silver coin weighing 58 grains and shaped like a cowrie. There is also another instance similar to this, known not from Indian epigraphy, but from Sanskrit literature. The word *hiraṇya* occurs in one of the aphorisms of Vātsyāyana's *Kāmasūtra.*[1] The commentator Śaṁkarārya explains this *hiraṇya* by *kapardaka*. Nay, the Sanskrit lexicon Medinī gives two senses of *hiraṇya*, one of which is *śātakumbha* or gold, and the other, *varāṭa* or cowrie. How can a word, which primarily signified 'gold,' come to signify also a 'cowrie' ? This cannot be taken

[1] VI. 5. 6. I am indebted to Prof. H. C. Chakladar for this reference.

to be an instance of the degradation of a word, for when a word is once degraded, it cannot express its original good sense side by side with its new derogatory meaning. The word *hiraṇya*, on the other hand, denotes both the senses, 'gold' and 'cowrie' in the period when Śaṁkarārya wrote or the lexicon Medinī was composed. We have, therefore, perforce to admit that when *kapardaka* is given as another word for *hiraṇya*, the former must be taken to signify a 'gold cowrie,' *i.e.* a gold coin shaped like a shell cowrie. *Hiraṇya* thus, according to the Medinī, signifies *śātakumbha*, *i.e.* gold (bullion) and *kapardaka*, *i.e.* (gold) cowries. In my last lecture, I had occasion to tell you in this connection that both the Egyptians and the Chinese had metallic representations of cowries as coins, and that there were actually gold cowries in the case of the former. Here then we have got two clear examples from India of metallic money being fashioned like a mineral product, *viz.* shell cowrie, which was the medium of exchange, and this could have taken place originally only when metallic currency first sprung into existence and was replacing as far as possible all the previous measures of value. It is true that the instances I have adduced are from the mediæval history of ancient India, but as I have already said, forms of money originating in the early stages of civilisation are preserved down to the historical periods. There can, therefore, be nothing unreasonable in supposing that gold and silver cowries came originally to be employed only when metallic currency was introduced but survived down to much later times in some parts of India at least.

Let us now see what denominations of coins were prevalent in the Vedic period. We have seen that the Ṛig-Veda speaks of *hiraṇya-piṇḍa* and Nishka. The former was not any regular coin, but was rather unstamped metallic bullion. The latter alone denotes a coin, and is also a coin denomination. Another denomination which is traceable in the Saṁhitā portion of the Vedic literature is Śatamāna. Reference to it occurs, as I have elsewhere told you, in the Taittirīya Saṁhitā. If Śatamāna was known in the Saṁhitā period, it stands to reason that it was known also in the Brāhmaṇa period. Thus that denomination is referred to not only in the Taittirīya but also in the Śatapatha Brāhmaṇa. What is, however, interesting in this connection to note, is that in the latter Brāhmaṇa, the Śatamāna is said to be not only of gold, but of *vṛitta* or round form. The same Brāhmaṇa speaks of a third class of coins called Suvarṇa which also is said to be of gold. Mention is made of a fourth denomination in the same work, I mean, Pāda, which I take to stand for one-fourth of the standard coin of that period.

Perhaps of the lowest denomination was Kṛishṇala, but it is not quite certain, though very probable, that it denoted a coin.[1] It will thus be seen that as many as five denominations of coins were known in the Vedic period and were all of gold, namely, Nishka, Śatamāna, Suvarṇa, Pāda and probably Kṛishṇala. It is only when we come to the post-Vedic epoch that we hear of another class of coins, namely, the Kārshāpaṇa. It is referred to along with the previous denominations not only in Pāṇini's Sūtras but also in the Jātaka literature, as I told you in my third lecture. But we find them all mentioned in the Manusaṁhitā (circa 150 B.C.) and the Yājñavalkya Smṛiti (circa 350 A.D.) which are the only two Smṛiti works that specify various kinds of old metallic stamped money.

I have again and again told you that names of coins are also names of metal weights, and the importance of these Smṛitis

---

[1] In this connection I may draw the attention of scholars to two thin pieces, one of gold and the other of silver, which were found in the Piprāwā Stūpa which is supposed to contain the remains of Buddha and which was probably of the 6th century B. C. The pieces are impressed with symbols and cannot therefore be looked upon as merely curious specimens of gold and silver foil. They no doubt each weigh a little over one grain. But we must note that the average weight of Kṛishṇalaka is 1·83 grains. May these have been intended for Kṛishṇalaka coins—an inference which agrees with the fact that coins have been found in all Buddhist Stūpas of importance and might have been conspicuous by their absence only in the Piprāwā Stūpa if these pieces had not been regarded as coins.

consists in the fact that the weight of each one of these denominations can be known in the terms of *krishṇalaka* or *guñjā* berries, and can thus be compared one with the other. Information on this point is to a certain extent supplied by Kauṭilya's Arthaśāstra, but it is almost nothing as compared to the detailed information given us by Manu. Of course, it is not to be expected that the condition of coinage that was prevalent in the Jātaka period or earlier was exactly the same as in the time when the Manusaṁhitā or the Yājñavalkya Smṛiti was composed. Thus Manu or Yājñavalkya would make us believe that Kārshāpaṇa was a copper coin only, whereas, as we have seen, it denoted silver and gold coinage also in the time of the Jātakas. Another point worth noting is that, according to Manu or Yājñavalkya, Śatamāna was a silver coin only, whereas, in the Brāhmaṇa period, it was also a gold coin. The typical silver coin, mentioned by Manu or Yājñavalkya, is Dharaṇa (also called Purāṇa by the former). But this Dharaṇa was equal to thirty Ratis or 90 White Mustard Seeds, whereas the Dharaṇa, mentioned by Kauṭilya, was equal to 88 of these Mustard Seeds. But the curious point here is the name Purāṇa which, as first noted by E. Thomas and Cunningham,[1] was looked upon as *purāṇa* or

[1] NChr., XIII (1873), p 211.

'ancient,' and must have come down to Manu's time from a hoary antiquity.

Whether these denominations of coins were all prevalent after 350 A.D., the date assigned to the Yājñavalkya Smṛiti, is doubtful. By the word "denomination" I do not simply mean the 'name,' but also the 'weight.' The mere name of a class of coins may survive down to a very late period, but the original denomination cannot be said to have been preserved, unless the 'weight' originally associated with the 'name' is also preserved. Let us, therefore, see how long after the middle of the fourth century A.D., the coins prevalent in the Vedic and Jātaka times persisted—how many in reality and how many in name only. Let us first take the Nishka coins. The word Nishka, some of you probably know, is met with in the Amarakosha which, I think, has to be ascribed to the fifth century A.D. But, in this lexicon, we are told that Nishka was another name for Dīnāra. Dīnāra, I have already informed you, was a coin struck by the Kushana kings in imitation of the Roman gold Denarius. Thus, the weight of a Dīnāra as of a Denarius was 124 grains, whereas that of a Nishka, according to Manu, was 560 grains. The Nishka of the Amarakosha could not, therefore, have been the same as the Nishka of the Manusaṁhitā. It will thus be seen that, in the fifth century A.D., we have merely the name Nishka preserved but not the original denomination. If this is the case with the fifth century, it must necessarily be true of the thirteenth and subsequent centuries. Thus we have got a South-Indian inscription of Śaka 1231,[1] where Gaṇḍamāḍa has been called a Nishka. This Gaṇḍamāḍa has in another inscription[2] been explained as a *māḍai* or coin of Gaṇḍagopāla which clearly shows that it cannot be identical with the Nishka of Manu. We thus perceive that the Nishka denomination mentioned in the Vedic and the Jātaka literature and detailed in the Manusaṁhitā had really gone out of vogue long before the fifth century A.D., though the mere name Nishka had been preserved up till the 14th century, to denote other coins. Not much different was the case with Śatamāna which is another gold denomination of the periods just referred to. For, we do not find any trace of this coin in literature or in inscriptions after the beginning of the Christian era. No doubt, that word occurs in the Amarakosha, but there is no evidence that this lexicon is here dealing with a class of coins actually prevalent at the time of its composition. In the case of Nishka, we have seen that the Amarakosha makes it synonymous with Dīnāra which was then in

---

[1] EI., V, 32 and 35, ll. 4 and 28. [2] *Ibid.*, VII. 131.

actual use. But there is no such evidence to show that by Śatamāna the Amarakosha is referring to some coin of its period. The mere occurrence of the word Śatamāna in this lexicon is, therefore, of no consequence, for lexicons have to take cognizance of all words whether there are any objects corresponding to them or not. Such was not, however, the case with Suvarṇa which is the third denomination of gold coins. For Suvarṇa we find actually referred to in one Nāsik cave inscription and at least one Gupta record.[1] In the case of the Gupta epigraph, it is, no doubt, possible to contend that, by Suvarṇa is probably intended the Dīnāra, which also we find mentioned in it. Just as the Amarakosha gives Nishka as another word for Dīnāra, it may be argued that the Gupta inscriptions may have used Suvarṇa also synonymously with Dīnāra. But it is worthy of note that we have two types of Gupta gold coins, one of which conforms to the weight of the Roman Denarius standard and the other to that of Manu's Suvarṇa.[2] We must, therefore, suppose that Dīnāra and Suvarṇa, which both occur in Gupta records, do not denote one identical but two different classes of coins. What the state of things was posterior to the Gupta period we do not know. Suvarṇas are

[1] EI., VIII. 82; GI., 265.

[2] CCGD., cxxxi and ff.

no doubt mentioned in epigraphs of later periods such, *e.g.*, as the Cambay copper-plate charter of the Rāshṭrakūṭa king Govinda IV,[1] dated 930 A.D. But we do not know whether they were of the weight attributed to that denomination by Manu. For, soon after the Gupta period, Suvarṇa certainly came to be identified with Dīnāra, as is clear from both Bṛihaspati and Kātyāyana Smṛitis.[2] I do not, however, maintain that the Suvarṇas of the Cambay copper-plate charter must denote Dīnāras, for it is very doubtful whether these gold Dīnāras were current so far south and so late as the tenth century. It is quite possible that just as Suvarṇa denoted a Dīnāra in the post-Gupta period in North India, it may have denoted some other gold coin in Gujarāt and the Dekkan.

We have now to consider the case of Kārshāpaṇa, and find out how long this kind of money lasted in ancient India. Let me here recapitulate a little of what I told you in Lecture III. Kārshāpaṇa, I hope you remember, was a class of coins, usually of silver and copper and weighing one Karsha. And as Kārshāpaṇas have been mentioned and described both in the Manu and Yājñavalkya Smṛitis, we may take it that this type of coinage continued till at least the fourth century A.D. Quite in keeping with

---

[1] EI., VII, p. 40, ll. 47 and 49.

[2] BS., No. 45, p. 231.

this inference is the fact that references to it are traceable in the West India cave inscriptions of the Śātavāhana period. Again, at Besnagar or ancient Vidiśā, I found punch-marked coins on all early sites containing strata reaching down to the fourth century A. D. But then, what about Kārshāpaṇa thereafter? Here the Bṛihaspati and Kātyāyana Smṛitis come to our aid.[1] Both these Smṛitis give Aṇḍikā as another name for Kārshāpaṇa, and a doubt is apt to arise in our mind as to whether this Kārshāpaṇa, which has such strange another name as Aṇḍikā, can really be the Kārshāpaṇa of Manu and Yājñavalkya. But be it noted that Bṛihaspati describes a Kārshāpaṇa as a stamped piece of copper which is one Karsha in weight. I am afraid it is not possible here to doubt that, by Kārshāpaṇa, Bṛihaspati understands precisely what Manu does. Again, look to the sub-divisions of the Kārshāpaṇa as detailed by Kātyāyana. A Kārshāpaṇa, says he, is equal to 20 Māshas, and a Māsha, which is also called Paṇa, is equal to 4 Kākaṇīs. In the first place, the terms Māsha and Kākaṇī employed by Kātyāyana to denote the sub-multiples of Kārshāpaṇa are precisely the terms used in the Jātakas and for the same purpose. Secondly, the table also is practically the same. That 4 Kākiṇīs make 1

[1] *Ibid.*, p. 231.

Māsha can be known also from the Jātakas. But Kātyāyana makes a Kārshāpaṇa equivalent to 20 Māshas, whereas Manu makes it equivalent to 16 Māshas. You may thus imagine a discrepancy here. But in Lecture III I told you that one Jātaka led us practically to infer that a Kārshāpaṇa equalled not 16 but 20 Māshas,[1] and that, what was still more important, a Pāda, according to the commentary on the Vinaya-Piṭaka, was equal to 5 Māshas, that is to say, a Kārshāpaṇa equalled 20 Māshas, at Rājagṛiha in the time of Bimbisāra. The tradition of the Kārshāpaṇa and its token money prevalent in the early Buddhist period was thus preserved so late as the 6th or 7th century A.D. as we find from Kātyāyana. No reasonable doubt can therefore be entertained as to Kārshāpaṇa having continued to circulate up to the 7th century. But then two points here deserve to be noticed. The first is that the Kārshāpaṇa described by Bṛihaspati and Kātyāyana denotes a copper coin only. This is exactly in consonance with what Manu says. In ancient times, however, Kārshāpaṇa denoted not only copper but also silver money. Is there any evidence, you may now ask, to show whether silver Kārshāpaṇa also was known in the mediæval period? I may, therefore, draw your attention

---

[1] *Supra*, pp. 111-2.

to the statement of Nārada that silver Kārshāpaṇa was current in South India.[1] And we no doubt find that the references to Kārshāpaṇa in the West India cave inscriptions are all to silver Kārshāpaṇa. Secondly, if the Kārshāpaṇa was certainly prevalent till the 7th century A.D., it could not have been represented at all periods by the punch-marked coins alone. There must have been some other types of coins which also were looked upon as Kārshāpaṇas. For no punch-marked coins later than the 4th century A.D., have been found so that between the 4th and the 7th century at any rate there must have been some type or types other than the punch-marked which were known as Kārshāpaṇa. Our history of the Kārshāpaṇa coinage is not yet over, for we have yet to consider the question whether Kārshāpaṇa was in any form known after the seventh century. An inscription originally found at Bijāpur[2] in the Goḍwāṛ Division of the Jodhpur State and dated 997 A.D., while recording the benefactions to a Jaina temple, speaks of a grant of one Karsha for every *ghaḍā* at every local oil-mill. As in the specification of similar grants in this connection the words Rūpaka and Viṁśopaka occur which denote coined money, it is difficult to avoid the inference that here Karsha stands for a copper

---

[1] BS., No. 45, p. 232.

[2] EI., X. 24 and 26-7.

Kārshāpaṇa. Similarly, the Gayā stone inscription of the Pāla king, Govindapāla,[1] dated V.E. 1232 (-1175 A.D.), makes mention of Kārshāpaṇī. It is not quite clear from this inscription whether this was a silver or copper Kārshāpaṇa, though there is greater likelihood in favour of the latter supposition. Of course, as, in the Bijāpur inscription, Kārshāpaṇa is denoted by the term *karsha* which is primarily the name of a weight, it must be taken as identical with the Kārshāpaṇa of Manu. But from the Gayā inscription itself, it is not possible to definitely assert that Kārshāpaṇī denoted the original Kārshāpaṇa denomination. It deserves, however, to be noted that such a word as *Kāhan* which is evidently the modern form of the Sanskrit Kārshāpaṇa has been preserved to this day in Bengal,[2] and that this Kāhan is valued at 16 Paṇas which, as I have already told you, is the same thing as Māshas. Every probability is, therefore, in favour of regarding the Kārshāpaṇī of the Gayā inscription as standing for the Kārshāpaṇa of the old metric system.

Now just one or two points before closing this history of the Kārshāpaṇa coinage. I have already stated on the authority of Kātyāyana that Māsha also known as Paṇa was not one-sixteenth but one-twentieth part of Kārshāpaṇa. Now, epigraphists need not be told that there

[1] *Pālas of Bengal*, p. 109.

[2] CAI., 43.

is such a coin as Viṁśopaka mentioned in inscriptions of the mediæval period and found in such provinces as Rājputānā, Central India and the Dekkan.[1] Numismatists have no doubt been telling us that it is one-twentieth part of some coin. But all this is vague information. Had we not rather say that it denoted the Paṇa or Māsha coin which forms one-twentieth part of Kārshāpaṇa?

Let me, again, draw your attention to what Bṛihaspati has said about Suvarṇa and Kārshāpaṇa. As I have told you, he identifies Suvarṇa with Dīnāra which, we know, weighs 124 grains, and takes Kārshāpaṇa to be a copper coin weighing one Karsha or 146·4 grains. Let us now see what metric connection he establishes between Kārshāpaṇa and Suvarṇa. According to him, 4 Kārshāpaṇas or Aṇḍakas make 1 Dhānaka, and 12 Dhānakas 1 Suvarṇa or Dīnāra. The same table is given by Kātyāyana also. The ratio of gold to copper in the early mediæval period, that is, when Bṛihaspati and Kātyāyana wrote, may be expressed thus: $146{\cdot}4 \times 4 \times 12 : 124 = 56{\cdot}7 : 1$. And the rate of exchange between the copper Kārshāpaṇa and the gold Dīnāra was 48 : 1. The present ratio between copper and gold is something like 1000 : 1. This, no doubt, shows that copper in early times had comparatively much greater value than it

[1] EI., I. 174, 176; II. 124, 240; III. 267; X. 19; XI. 41, 56.

possesses at present, almost at twenty times as much as now. Perhaps this calculation may not at once convince you. But let me tell you that, in the provinces where Dīnāra was current, no silver coinage was in existence, I mean, in the dominions of the Kushanas and their successors, the Guptas. From the economic point of view, such a thing would not have been possible, if copper had not been of such high value at that period as to dispense with the necessity of any silver coinage.

That copper was of much higher value in ancient India than at present is evident in another way also. In Lecture III, I informed you that, in some places, such as Vidiśā, there was nothing but copper currency only. How is this possible except on the supposition that copper possessed much greater value than now? For what was then the standard money at Vidiśā? It was the copper Kārshāpaṇa, as I told you. Kārshāpaṇa, we know, contained sixteen Māshas or Paṇas, and each Paṇa, according to the Līlāvatī, was valued at 80 cowries. Again, a Kārshāpaṇa, we know, was equal to 80 Ratis or Guñjās in weight. Here then we have got a standard copper coin, namely, Kārshāpaṇa, which is 80 Guñjās in weight, and is, in value, equal to 80×16=1280 cowries. Take now the modern pice which weighs 48 Guñjās. Its value in cowries however differs in different provinces.

But let us take the highest value it had in modern times, *viz.* 64 cowries in Mahārāshṭra. A Kārshāpaṇa thus becomes equivalent to 20 modern pice, that is, five annas, although its weight is not even double that of a pice! Perhaps you may now say: granted that copper had much higher value than at present as no doubt this calculation shows, but how can any town or province have the highest denomination of coins which equals only five annas? And I may, therefore, tell you that in Cutch to this day the highest denomination known as Kori is about 4 annas only in worth!

A short while ago, I drew your attention to certain information contained in the later Smṛitis, which enables us to fix the ratio between gold and copper. You may now be curious to know whether we have any data to determine the ratio between gold and silver at any period in ancient India. While giving the history of the Suvarṇa coinage posterior to the time of Manu, I had occasion to tell you that there was one Nāsik cave inscription,[1] which contained a reference to this denomination. We are there informed of a certain grant of 70,000 Kārshāpaṇas, which, we are expressly told, were equal to 2000 Suvarṇas, at the rate of 35 (silver) Kārshāpaṇas to 1 Suvarṇa. All these items of information have been given in so many words,

[1] EI., VIII. 82.

leaving no scope at all for any surmise. Of course, the Kārshāpaṇas here referred to are the silver coins of that name. The weight of a silver Kārshāpaṇa or Purāṇa, we know, is 58·5 and that of Suvarṇa is 146·4 grains. And as the exchange rate between Kārshāpaṇa and Suvarṇa was 35 : 1, we get the following calculation: $58{\cdot}5 \times 35 : 146{\cdot}4 = 14 : 1$ approximately. The ratio of gold to silver was thus 14:1 in the second century A.D.[1] which comes very nearly to that of the modern times.

So much about the denominations of coins, their weights, and their persistence to the late mediæval period. But what did the coins of the Jātaka, if not of the Vedic period, look like? In other words, how were their obverse and reverse? This is the question that you are sure to ask me now, and I shall therefore attempt to give a reply which appears most likely to me. Of course, we shall first have to turn our attention to the Kārshāpaṇas. I have already told you what sort of devices are to be found on these coins. I have also told you that in the earlier class, these devices occur in a haphazard unconnected manner, but that, in their later development, they appear in definite and constant groups, though each symbol is stamped with a separate punch. A further development on this

[1] This practically agrees with the ratio (15 : 1) mentioned by the Marāṭhī poet, Jñāneśvar, as being current in Mahārāshṭra in his time, *i.e.* in the thirteenth century A.D.

class is marked by coins where these constant and regular groups are impressed on them with a single die and not with different punches. I have only to refer you to the coins of the Gaṇas, such as Mālava and Yaudheya, of the Janapadas, such as Śibi and Rājanya, of such royal dynasties as the Śātavāhanas, and of such countries as those of Mathurā and Pañchāla. All the coins, native to these provinces and peoples and ranging in date roughly from the third century B.C. to 3rd century A.D., are characterized with a collection of symbols forming one distinct type and struck from a single die. As all the symbols occurring on these coins are such as are commonly found on the Kārshāpaṇas, no reasonable doubt can be entertained as to their constituting indigenous money. Of course, not a few of them are of round shape, but this need not be looked upon as betokening foreign—Greek—influence. For even some Kārshāpaṇas have been found to be of circular form, and, as you will remember, Śatamānas have been called *vṛitta* or round in the Śatapatha Brāhmaṇa. It is not, therefore, permissible to have any reasonable doubt in regard to the indigenous character of these coins. Obviously this class of money has been evolved from the Kārshāpaṇa. When exactly this development took place is not known. It is true that the Kārshāpaṇas are traceable to the prehistoric period. But because they have come down from this hoary antiquity, it does not necessarily prove that its latest development represented by the coins just adverted to must also have taken place at that early period. Those coins, I have just informed you, belong to a period ranging from between 300 B.C. and 300 A.D. And we shall not be far from right if we assign this latest evolution of the indigenous money to the 5th or 6th century B.C. The circulation of these coins side by side with the Kārshāpaṇas need not distract us. For, at the beginning of this lecture, I have iterated and re-iterated that forms of currency originating at different stages of civilisation were prevalent side by side in a comparatively modern epoch. We thus get a pretty fair idea of the appearance that must have been presented by indigenous coins in the Jātaka period.

Of course, the Kārshāpaṇa type too must have its history of evolution, and it does not seem very difficult to surmise the steps in which it came to evolve itself. Kārshāpaṇa, you know, is a coin of various shapes, such as rectangular, circular, elongated and even irregular, and is impressed with devices of various kinds. Nobody, therefore, can doubt Kārshāpaṇa as denoting a distinct coinage. The earliest stage of coinage in India is represented by *hiraṇya-piṇḍas* or unstamped buttons of metal passing for currency. These *hiraṇya-piṇḍas* must have conformed to a definite size and weight. But where was the guarantee of the purity of their metal or of their definite value ? A time must, therefore, have come when it was thought necessary to relieve men of the trouble of testing their quality, and, therefore, the natural step of setting a stamp on every coin to guarantee fineness of metal is easy to conceive. Coins pertaining to this stage of monetary development are represented, I think, by solid silver ingots with three circular dots on one side and also silver bent bars with one or two symbols on one face only such as we find described by V. A. Smith in his *Catalogue*. This stamp evidently must have acted as a kind of hall-mark. The further development of this coinage to a full-fledged Kārshāpaṇa it is easy to surmise. The devices must have soon come to be multiplied indefinitely and not one face but both the faces of the coin must gradually have come to be stamped with these, the reverse symbol in most cases representing the badge of the controlling authority. Steps must also have been taken for the establishment of a regular shape to prevent any tampering with coin after its manufacture. And this is the reason probably why we see Kārshāpaṇas of so many shapes which appear to me to be so many experiments in form. It is possible further to conceive that the devices were first punched on the obverse in a haphazard fashion, but were afterwards impressed in regular and constant groups, as I have told you so many times, to indicate the provenance of the coin. The further development of the Kārshāpaṇa into a regular and distinct coin type struck from a die I have already dilated upon, and so scarcely requires any repetition here.

You will thus see in what successive stages the coinage of Ancient India most probably evolved itself and what actual type was prevalent in the fifth or sixth century B.C. This last, as I have told you, is the one perceptible in the indigenous money of the Gaṇas, Janapadas, royal dynasties, and such provinces as Mathurā and Pañchāla. This date does not seem to be too early. For you have only to take into consideration some of the earliest coins of this type. Take, for instance, the coin, which bears the legend *Vaṭasvaka* and which, according to Cunningham, is anterior to the Greek conquest of Alexander, but which, Bühler thinks it safe to say, is anterior to the Greek conquest of Demetrius.[1] What do we find on the obverse of this coin, which alone is stamped? We find not only the legend in Brāhmī character, but a hill symbol with a standing figure to right,

---

[1] No. III, p. 48.

beneath which is a sign called Nandipada. There is also a pile of balls or dots beneath the hill. It is scarcely necessary for me to remark that all these symbols are found on Kārshāpaṇa coins. But the point to note here is that all these devices form one type and have been struck with a single die. And if this Vaṭasvaka coin belongs to the third century B.C., at the latest, there is nothing irrational in pushing the origin of such a type back to the fifth or sixth century.

The type of coins which has been described is, as I have informed you, evolved from the Kārshāpaṇa. But you will naturally want to know whether there was any other type prevalent in this early period. It is, therefore, necessary to invite your attention to some more coins. I hope you have not forgotten the coins of the autonomous cities of the Punjab to which I have referred in my first lecture. On the obverse occurs the word *negamā*, and on the reverse, such names as Dojaka Tālimata and Atakatakā.[1] I had then occasion to tell you that the word *negamā* here must be taken to signify 'the city people' and that the letters occurring on the reverse must be understood to be the names of the cities. What is noteworthy here is that on neither of the faces of these coins

---

[1] CL., 1918, pp. 75-6.

occurs anything but the legend. They are conspicuous by the absence of any kind of symbols, such as we are accustomed to note on the Kārshāpaṇa. It thus appears that in that early period, some coins were struck with mere names unaccompanied by any devices. If further evidence is required, it is supplied by a coin found at Eraṇ in the Central Provinces. On this coin only one legend occurs and on one face only, the legend consisting of the letters *Raño Dhammapālasa* in very ancient Brāhmī characters.[1] And as these characters run from right to left, Bühler thinks that they could not have been later than the fifth century B. C.[2] This coin is thus earlier than those of the autonomous cities of the Punjab, and, as we have just seen, is devoid of all devices, and has been found in one of the Eastern Provinces of India. It will not, therefore, be unreasonable if we infer that another type of coinage which was prevalent at this early period and which was in no way influenced by the Kārshāpaṇa consisted of mere legends stamped on one or both sides.

So far in regard to the denominations of coins indigenous to India, that is say, those handed down from the Vedic and the pre-Buddhistic period. Let me now say a few words on the new designations of monetary value that

---

[1] Al., 151.

[2] IS., No. III, pp. 44-7.

sprang up after the Greek domination of North-west India. It is not my object here to give a history of the coinages of these foreign dynasties, or those of even Indian dynasties influenced by theirs. So much has already been written upon the coins of the Indo-Bactrian Greek, Indo-Scythian, and Indo-Parthian dynasties, and their Indian successors, the Guptas and others, that there is hardly anything new for me to tell. I will therefore, confine myself here, briefly of course, to the new denominations that arose, that is to say, the denominations unknown to Manu and Yājñavalkya. It is curious that, in spite of the fact that the Indo-Bactrian Greeks had their own coinage struck according to the Attic Standard, names technical to Hellenic metrology were unknown to India up till the second century A.D., when, as I have told you already, their power must have become extinct. It is when the Kushanas rise to power that we find not one but two new denominations springing up. The first is Kuśaṇa,[1] which occurs in a Nāsik cave inscription, recording a grant of Ushavadāta, son-in-law of the Kshatrapa Nahapāna, who ruled over South Rājputānā, Gujarāt and North Dekkan, about the close of the first and the beginning of the second century A.D. Ushavadāta, we are told, deposited a sum of

[1] IA., 1918, p. 76 and ff.

1000 Kārshāpaṇas, at the monthly rate $\frac{3}{4}$ per cent., and yielding, therefore, an annual interest of 90 Kārshāpaṇas. This amount of 90 Kārshāpaṇas, the inscription says, was the Kuśaṇamūla, *i.e.* the value of Kuśaṇas. Looking, however, to the similar phraseology used in other cave inscriptions of this period, I have shown elsewhere that Kuśaṇa of this, must correspond to Paḍika (= Pratika) of other, cave epigraphs, and must denote a specific coin. And I have further ventured to express the view that Kuśaṇa in particular denotes the silver coinage of Nahapāna, and was so called, because he issued it for his Kuśaṇa or Kushana overlord who must have been Kadphises I. I have just told you that Ushavadāta deposited a sum of 1000 Kārshāpaṇas in a guild which annually yielded 90 Kārshāpaṇas by way of interest. This inscription was engraved in Ushavadāta's cave which accommodated 20 monks and where each of them was to be given a Kuśaṇa for every one of the four months of the rainy season. Evidently, therefore, 80 Kuśaṇas were required every year, and had to be obtained with the 90 Kārshāpaṇas, the annual interest just referred to. We thus see that 80 Kuśaṇas were equivalent to 90 Kārshāpaṇas, or, in other words, the rate of exchange between these two classes of coins was 8 : 9.

The next designation of monetary value that we have to consider is Dīnāra. I have again and again told you that it was the name of the gold coins introduced by the Kushana kings and continued by the Gupta sovereigns and that Dīnāra was so called after the Roman Denarius. There were, however, two kinds of Denarius, *viz.* gold and silver, and it was the former, that is, *Denarius aureus* of about 122 grains, that was adopted, by the Kushana rulers, for their gold coins. It was for this reason that only the gold coins of the Kushanas and the Guptas are designated Dīnāras, no silver Dīnāras being yet known. Now, the question here arises: why did the Kushanas adopt the Roman standard of weight for their coins? Does it not indicate that there was brisk trade going on between Rome and India? Of course, this trade had begun long prior to the reign of Augustus, for do we not know that silver denarii of the Consular period have been found in Stūpas on the north-west frontiers of India?[1] It is worthy of note that Roman coins have been found in India in abandance and that they are generally found in two regions, namely, (1) in the north-west, and (2) in and near the Coimbatore District and at Madura in the Madras Presidency. Those picked up in South India pertain to the period commencing with Augustus and ending with the

[1] The greater portion of the information given here is based upon Sewells' article *Roman Coins found in India* (JRAS., 1904, p. 591 and ff.).

death of Nero, that is, from 27 B.C. to 68 A.D. Hoards of Roman coins belonging to this period are reported to have been discovered in this region. It is not difficult to find out the cause of it. Pliny, writing about A.D. 70, laments the wasteful extravagance of the richer classes and their reckless expenditure on spices, pepper, perfumes, ivory, fine muslins, cotton and precious stones, such as the beryl. Most of these exports to Rome, I need scarcely point out, are products of South India. And, in particular, I may draw your attention to the Beryl stone which was most highly prized in Rome. This beryl is found in India in one place only, namely, Padyur in the Coimbatore District. And, curiously enough, it is in the neighbourhood of its mines that the largest number of Roman coins of this period have been found. With the reign of Vespasian, things seem to have changed. For what with his exemplary life and what with enactments he succeeded in largely suppressing the wanton extravagance and profligacy of the age. And the tides probably turned against India. For it was in the period beginning with the death of Nero (A.D. 68) and ending with Caracalla (A.D. 217), that we see not only the issue of gold coinage by the Kushanas, but, above all, their adoption of the Roman standard of weight. Cunningham, V. A. Smith and Professor Rapson concur in the belief that the Kushana kings recoined the Roman *aurei*. This means that they got hold of all Roman gold coins, melted them down in a mass, and issued their own coins of precisely the same weight. This supposition, however, does not commend itself to me. For, in the first instance, I cannot understand why all the Roman coins, the gold and not the copper, were so treated. Secondly, if the Kushana coins are nothing but the Roman coins melted and restruck, the latter must have come to India in proportionately huge quantities. As a matter of fact, however, the Roman copper coins are conspicuous by their paucity. Thirdly, if the Kushana rulers melted the Roman gold coins, why did they strike new coins of their own of exactly the same weight as the Roman? I am inclined to believe that the Kushana kings adopted the Roman standard of weight to facilitate trade, as the Roman coin was accepted almost all over the world at this time. But the fact that very few Roman gold coins of this period have been found in North India shows that the trade was against India, that is to say, the exports from the Roman Empire preponderated over those from India. Evidently, therefore, the Kushana gold coins must on the contrary have been imported into the Roman Empire. It is scarcely necessary to remind you that coins of Kanishka have been dug up in such remotest parts of Europe as Scandinavia and Wales,[1] and I have no doubt that more Kushana coins will be found in Europe and West Asia when we excavate sites of this period.

How long the Dīnāra denomination lasted in India we do not know. Certainly it continued to circulate till the early mediæval period, that is, the seventh century A.D., when the Bṛihaspati and Kātyāyana Smṛitis were compiled. For we have already seen that these law books make specific mention of Dīnāra as a synonym of Suvarṇa. Of about the same age is an inscription at Bodh Gayā, which speaks of the plastering and whitewashing of the temple at the cost of 250 Dīnāras. For the reasons adduced by T. Bloch, the well-known gold coins of Gupta mintage are meant here by the Dīnāras.[2] In the late mediæval period, however, the word was used in the sense of coined money or cash. It thus ceased to be the designation of any particular monetary value. The Rājataraṅgiṇī, *e.g.*, which has to be ascribed to the 11th century A.D., speaks of 'dīnnāras' of gold, silver and copper.[3] Dīnāras are also mentioned not only in round hundreds and thousands but also lakhs and crores, so as to make it manifestly

[1] JRAS., 1912, p. 672.

[2] ASI.—AR., 1908-9, pp. 153-54.

[3] Stein's *Kalhaṇa's Chronicles of the Kings of Kashmir*, II. 308-9.

impossible for Dīnāra to be any gold or even silver coin.

Another designation of coined money of a somewhat later period than Dīnāra is Kedāra. In my Lecture IV, I hope you remember I had occasion to quote a passage from the Kāśikā which speaks of Dīnāra, Kedāra, and Kārshāpaṇa as *rūpya* or coined money. Of course, you know what coins are denoted by Dīnāra and Kārshāpaṇa. But what is a Kedāra? This question I am sure you will ask me here. I am afraid I cannot give any reply that is positively convincing. But let me here draw your attention to the coins of the Kidāra-Kushanas. These coins have been found in Kāshmīr and some parts of Gandhāra, and the Kidāra-Kushanas themselves are supposed to have held power from 425 to 900 A.D. What deserves to be noticed here is that all the coins have the name Kidāra on the obverse. This Kidāra has been identified by Cunningham with *Ki-to-lo*, the leader of the great Yuch-ti, known from Chinese sources.[1] What the real significance of Kidāra is we do not definitely know. But this appears to be almost certain that the Kedāra of the Kāśikā is to be connected with the Kidāra of the Little Kushana coins. Most probably the coin Kedāra was called after this Kidāra dynasty.

---

[1] *Ibid.*, II. 319-20; IC., 19-20.

We now come to the denomination Dramma which was prevalent all over North India up to the Narmadā in the late mediæval period, that is, from the ninth to the thirteenth century A.D. The earliest record, where this word has been traced, is the Gwalior inscription of Bhojadeva of the Imperial Pratīhāra dynasty and dated 875 A.D.[1] Obviously the word Dramma has to be traced to the Greek Drachma. But it is curious that although the Greeks ruled over North-West India from 200 B.C. to 200 A.D., the word is not to be found in any literature or epigraphic record of that period. It is really not till the middle of the ninth century that we hear of this word at all. This clearly shows that the influence of the Indo-Bactrian Greeks over Indian political and economic life was not very deep. How then did the word *Dramma* arise, and, above all, in the late mediæval period? The explanation of it has to be found, I think, in the invasion of the Gurjaras who appear to have strongly imbibed the Sassanian civilisation, though perhaps not ethnologically connected with them. The Drachma of the Greeks was prevalent in Iran

[1] The views here expressed in regard to the denomination of Dramma were first made known by me to the Ancient Indian Numismatics class of the Calcutta University in 1919. And it is particularly gratifying to find almost the same views expressed by such a veteran numismatist as Prof. Rapson before the joint session of orientalists in London (JRAS., 1920, pp. 151-2).

till the Sassanian period, and the Gurjaras, who poured into India in the 6th or 7th century A.D., must evidently have come from there. What are called the Indo-Sassanian coins by the numismatists were, in my opinion the earliest issues of these Gurjaras. I have elsewhere shown how far the Gurjara might extended. Certainly it had spread as far east as Bengal and as far south as the Narmadā. And the Sassanian characteristics, which are clear and indisputable on their early issues, can be traced on all coins, gold, silver and copper, up to almost the thirteenth century A.D., though the original fabric and type gradually change.

The weight of a Dramma has been found to approximate to 65 grains. Indeed, there are Drammas which weigh even less than 60 grains. This diminution of weight may be explained exactly in the manner in which we explained divergence of weight in the case of Kārshāpaṇa. It is, therefore, quite correct to say that the standard weight of Dramma comes to 65 grains, whereas the Greek Drachma weighs only 66 grains. The difference is so insignificant that it may be safely neglected. It was this standard of weight, according to which gold, silver and copper coins were struck. The name Dramma was, however, restricted to the silver class only, the copper class being generally known as *Gadhaiyā-kā-paisā*. Various rulers of this period issued Drammas which are therefore named after them. We have thus Śrīmad-Ādivarāha-dramma called after Bhoja-Ādivarāha of the Pratīhāra dynasty,[1] Vigrahapālīya-dramma (also Vigrahatuṅgīya-dramma) supposed to be named after Vigrahapāla of the Pāla dynasty,[2] and Ajayadeva-dramma struck by Ajayadeva [3] the Chauhān king, who founded the city of Ajmer in Rājputānā. Of course, there were other kinds of Drammas which apparently were not connected with the name of any king. Such, *e.g.*, is the Pañchiyaka-dramma, which is mentioned in the Sīyaḍoṇī inscription.[4] What the meaning of the word *Pañchiyaka* is we cannot for certain tell. Possibly it denoted the coinage struck by the local Pañchāyat. What, however, we are here concerned with is that the denomination Dramma, which denoted a silver coin and was in imitation of the Sassanian coinage, was prevalent in India in the mediæval period. Of the same period are copper coins which are commonly known as *Gadhāiyā-kā-paisā.* That they also are imitations of the Sassanian originals is indisputable. And the only names that have so far been traced on them are Śrī-Chhittarāja[5] who has been identified with the Chhittarāja of the Silāhāra dynasty

---

[1] EI., I. 175. 27 and 178. 11.

[2] EI., I. 174.13, 175. 28, 176. 14, and 177. 10; AS R. XI. 175 and 181; CMI. 51-2.

[3] IA., 1912, 209.

[4] EI., I. 173.23; 178.12.

[5] JRAS., 1900, pp. 118 and 122.

of Ṭhāṇā, and Śrī-Somaladevī,[1] Queen of the Chauhān king Ajayadeva. Gold coins of the same weight standard were issued by some royal dynasties of the mediæval period such as Kalachuris, the Chandellas, the Gāhaḍavālas and so forth. How they were exactly designated in that period we do not know. But there is an inscription in a Kaṇherī cave of the time of the Rāshṭrakūṭa king, Amoghavarsha,[2] which speaks of Kāñchana-Drammas, which must, I think, stand for these gold coins. I have already mentioned that in the Cambay copper-plate charter of Govinda IV, Suvarṇas have been referred to. In inscriptions and literature of this period, we find mention also made of Nishkas. It appears that both Suvarṇas and Nishkas denoted Kāñchana-Drammas during the mediæval period. How the copper coins of this weight standard were designated at that time we do not know. In modern parlance, they are called *Gadhaiyā-kā-paisā*, as I have just told you.

What about the sub-divisions of this Dramma denomination? Were any known at this period? I have in this connection to refer you to the Sīyaḍoṇī inscription, which speaks of no less than two such sub-divisions, namely, Pāda and Viṃśopaka. Thus we find mentioned

[1] IA., 1912, p. 211.
[2] *Ibid.*, XIII. 186.

Pañchiyaka-dramma-satka-pāda and Śrīmad-Ādi-varāha-drammasya Pāda[1] on the one hand, and Varāhakīya-viṃśopaka, Vigraha-dramma-viṃśopaka and Bhîmapriya Viṃśopaka[2] on the other. Of course, Pāda must denote here one-fourth of the Dramma by whomsoever it was struck, and Viṃśopaka one-twentieth part thereof. What is worthy of note is that both denote specific coins. As a matter of fact, we do find coins of the mediæval dynasties which are one-fourth, as there are some which are one-half, of the weight of the Dramma. The first class is evidently intended here by the designation Pāda. There is, however, no silver or gold coin which is one-twentieth part of the weight. I, therefore, suspect that Viṁśopaka signifies a copper piece which is one-twentieth part in value of the original dramma. If this surmise is a likely one, we have to suppose that Viṁśopaka denotes a Paṇa or Māsha according, however, to the table of Kātyāyana which makes a Māsha or Paṇa as one-twentieth part of Kārshāpaṇa in value. The Kārshāpaṇa of this table must evidently stand for a silver coin, and is probably another name for Dramma. This class of Kārshāpaṇa, as Kātyāyana tells us, was prevalent in the Punjab, and we may take it also

---

[1] EI., I. 173. 28; 178. 11.

[2] *Ibid.*, I. 174. 10; 176. 24; XI. 59.

in Rājputānā and Gujarāt, and must in no way be confounded with the copper Kārshāpaṇa mentioned by Kātyāyana immediately afterwards as a synonym for Aṇḍikā and as being one-fourth of Dhānaka.[1]

---

[1] BS., No. 45, p. 231; compare this with the quotation from Kātyāyana given by Hemādri in *Chaturvaga-chintāmaṇi*, Vol. II, pt. I, p. 55 (Bibli. Ind. Ed.).

ANCIENT INDIAN WEIGHTS FROM MANU AND YÂJÑAVALKYA.

Table No. 1.

Estimated weights in grs. Troy.

Estimated weight				
	Silver.			
3·5	2 Rati = 1 Māshaka			
56·0	32 „ = 16 „	= 1 Dharaṇa or Purāṇa.		
560·0	320 „ = 160 „	= 10 „	= 1 Satamāna.	
	Gold.			
8·75	5 Rati = 1 Māsha			
140·0	80 „ = 16 „	= 1 Suvarṇa		
560·0	320 „ = 64 „	= 4 „	= 1 Pala or Nishka	
5600·0	3200 „ = 640 „	= 40 „	10 Pala or Nishka = 1 Dharaṇa	
	Copper.			
140·0	80 Rati = 1 Kārshāpaṇa			

Table No. 2.

Estimated weights in grs. Troy.

Estimated weight					
·00135		Trasareṇu			
·01080	8	„	= 1 Likhyā or Likshyā		
·03240	24	„	= 3 „	= 1 Rājasarshapa	
·0972	72	„	= 9 „	= 3 „	= 1 Gaura-sarshapa
·5833	432	„	= 54 „	= 18 „	= 6 Gaura-sarashapa = 1 Yava
1·75	1296	„	= 162 „	= 54 Rājasarshapa = 18 Gaurasarshapa = 3 Yava = 1 Kṛishṇala or Rati	

INDEX

A

Abdagases, Indo-Parthian ruler, 3.
Abhīras, 27.
Agathocles, coins of, 35, 143.
Ajayadeva-dramma, coin of the Chauhan King Ajayadeva, 208-09.
Akhæmenid Persian coinage, 118, 121.
Akshapaṭala, 126.
Alexander, 12, 24-7, 29-33, 144, 149, 196.
Amarakosha, 22-3, 82-3, 133-34, 181-83.
Amarasiṁha, the lexicographer, 82-3, 86.
Amoghavarsha, the Rāshṭrakūṭa king, 209.
Amyntas, coins of, 35.
Anantpur district (S. India), lead coins found in, 143.
Anāthapiṇḍika, 149.
Aṇḍaka, another name for Kārshāpaṇa, 189. See also *Aṇḍika*.
Andhrabhṛitya dynasty, lead and potin coins issued by, 141, 145.
Andhradeśa, lead coins found in, 143.
Aṇḍika, another name for Kārshāpaṇa, 185, 211. See also *Aṇḍaka*.
Antialkidas, coins of, 33, 40.
Antimachus II, coins of, 40.
Antiochus Theos, Syrian Emperor, 26, 41.
Ardha-Kārshāpaṇa, 77, 113.
Ardha-Māshaka, 77, 79, 90, 112.
Arrian, the Greek historian, 32.
Artemis, the Greek goddess as a coin-type, 35.
Arthaśāstra of Kauṭilya, 5, 87, 89, 90, 92, 112, 125, 126, 129, 156, 160, 180.
Ashṭādhyāyī of Pāṇini, 45, 47, 170.
Aśoka, inscriptions of, 25-6.
Assyrio-Babylonian weight, 121-22.

Atharvaveda, 64, 172.
Athena, the Greek goddess as a coin-type, 27.
Athens, coin-types of, 27-8.
Attic standard, 41, 199.
Augustus, 201.
Azes I, the Indo-Scythian prince, 3, 7, 8 ;
—lead coins of, 142-3.
Azes II, the Indo-Scythian prince, 3, 7.
Azilises, the Indo-Scythian prince, 3, 7, 8.

B

Babbu-Jātaka, 80.
Babylonians, the, 38-9, 42.
Bactria, Greek rule in, 25-6, 41.
Bactrian Greek coins, 41.
Ballāla Sena, his Naihāti grant, 139.
Bayley, Sir E. C., 40.
Bel ium, nickel pieces of, 143.
Bengal, practice of making necklaces out of coins in, 67.
Besnagar, 85, 98-100, 112, 114, 118, 185.
Bhagavadgītā, Mārāṭhī commentary on it by Jñānadeva, 147.
Bhagwanlal Indraji, Pandit, 9-10, 105.
Bhandarkar, Sir Ramkrishna, 24-5, 46.
Bhārhut, 149.
Bhāvayavya, a Vedic king, 64.
Bhoja-Ādivarāha, the Pratihāra king, 208.
Bhojadeva, Gwalior inscription of, 206.
Bhuridatta-Jātaka, 50-1.
Bijāpur, inscriptions found at, 187-88.
Bimbisāra, 111, 186.
Black Yajurveda, 58.
Bloch, Dr. T., 204.
Bodh Gayā inscription, 204.
Bodhisatta, 48, 52.
Böhtlingk, Prof., 59.
Brāhmaṇas, reference to coins in, 56, 60, 70.
Brāhmī, 38, 43, 136, 196, 198.
Bṛihaspati Smṛiti, 184-86, 189, 204.
Bṛihatsaṁhitā, 13.
Buddha, 16, 125, 130.

Buddhaghosha, 99, 126, 128, 132, 140-42, 145-47, 159, 160.
Bühler, 42, 46, 125-26, 149, 154, 196, 198.
Bull emblem of Śiva on the coins of Mihirakula, 18.
Burma, metals chopped to a certain weight used as a medium of exchange up till the advent of the British in, 61-2, 170, 173.
Burmese silver shells, 136.
Burnouf, 104.

C

Caldwell, 109.
Cambay Copper-plate of Govinda IV, 183, 209.
Caracalla, 202.
Cartailhac, 104.
Champeyya Jātaka, 50.
Chandā district, potin coins issued by the Andhra-Bhṛityas in, 145.
Chandellas, gold coins of, 209.
Chandragupta, the founder of the Maurya dynasty, 26, 30.
Chandragupta I, the founder of the Gupta dynasty, 9, 10.
Chashṭana, a Kshatrapa, ruler of Western India, 4, 18, 145.
Chatur-Māshaka, 77, 87, 90, 112.
Chhāṁdogya Upanishad, 55-6.
Chinese bronze cowries, 136, 139.
Chitaldrug district, lead coins found in, 143.
Chitorgaḍh, 13.
Chittarāja, a Silāhāra king, 208.
Collegiate Sovereignty, types of, 5.
Coromandel coast, lead coins found in, 143.
Cuddapah district, lead coins found in, 143.
Cunningham, Sir Alexander, 11, 38, 41-2, 86-9, 94-5, 98, 105, 107, 109, 143-44, 148-49, 157, 162, 180, 196, 202, 205.
Cutch, Kori coinage of, 191.
Cyzicus, coinage of, 6, 137-38.

D

Dāmaysada, Kshatrapa ruler, 19.
Dāms, Moghul copper coins, 117-18, 161.
Daric, 119.
Decourdemanche, M. J. A., 118, 120-22.

Dekkan, the, 147, 184, 189.
Demetrius, 35, 149, 196.
Denarius, Roman gold coin, 181, 201.
Ḍhābuās, unstamped copper coins, 70.
Dhānaka, a class of coins, 189, 211.
Dharaṇas, Purāṇas known as, 92-3, 180.
Didrachmas, 119.
Die-struck coins, 40.
Dīnāras, a class of gold coins, 67, 131, 133, 181-84, 189-90, 200-01, 204-05.
Diodotos, 26, 41.
Dionysios, the reputed founder of the city of Nysa, 32 ;
—identified with Śiva, 35.
Divodās, a Vedic King, 69.
Drachma, 206-07.
Dramma, a coin-denomination, 206-10.
Dvi-Māshaka, 77, 90.

E

Edakal, rock-carvings in, 107.
Eggeling, Prof., 57.
Egyptian gold representation of cowries, 139.
Eka-Māshaka, 77, 90.
Elliot, W., 108, 110, 142.
Erān, 100, 198.
Eucratides, square bronze coins of, 33.
Euthydemus, coins of, 143.

F

Fergusson, 108.
Fleet, Dr. J. F., 9.
Flight, Dr. Walter, 143-44.

G

Gadhāiyā-kā-paisā, a class of copper coins, 207-09.
Gāhaḍavālas, gold coins of, 209.
Gāmaṇīchaṇḍa Jataka, 77,

Gaṇa, an oligarchy, 5, 13, 152, 193, 196.
Gaṇanā, 124-28.
Gaṇḍagopāla, 182.
Gaṇḍamāḍa, a coin of Gaṇḍagopāla, 182.
Gāndhāra, 26, 116, 205.
Gaudhāras, the, referred to in the Aśoka inscriptions, 25.
Gautama, 82.
Gautamiputra Yajña-Śrī-Śatākarṇi, 85.
Gaura Sarshapa, a standard of weight, 93.
Gayā stone inscription of Govindapāla, 188.
Golakhpur (Patna), find spot of 108 punch-marked coins, 98.
Goldstücker, Prof., 24-5, 46.
Gondophares, founder of the Indo-Parthian dynasty, 3, 14, 19.
Gopatha Brāhmaṇa, 63.
Go-puchcha, used as a circulating medium in Pāṇini's time, 169-70.
Govinda IV, the Rāshṭrakūṭa king, 184, 209.
Govindapāla, Gayā stone inscription of, 188.
Greek cites, coinages of, 6.
Greek colony in India, 29, 31-2.
Greek deities on Kushana coins, 15.
Greek kings mentioned in the Aśoka inscriptions, 25.
Greek coinage, possibility of Indian coinage being imitated from it, 38, 40-1.
Guḍimallam Liṅga, 20.
Gupta gold coins, two types of, 183.
Gupta period, absence of gold coins of genuinely Indian type prior to it, 91, 94-5.
Guptas, the, 85, 88, 190, 199, 201, 204.
Gurjaras, the, 27, 206-07.
Gwalior inscription of Bhojadeva, 206.

H

Hairaṇyika, a goldsmith, 147, 160.
Hāthigumphā cave inscription, 127.
Hekate, the three-headed Greek divinity, 35,
Heliodorus, a *Bhāgavata*, ambassador from Antialkidas to Kāshiputra Bhāgabhadra, 33.
Hellenic deities, 32-6.
Hemchandra Roy Chowdhury, 32.
Herakles, identified with Kṛishṇa or Balarāma, 35.

Hermaeus, coins of, 35.
Hindu deities on Kushana coins, 15.
Hiraṇaya, a class of gold coins, 50-1, 176-77.
Hiraññā, gold pieces mentioned in the Jātakas, 80.
Hiraṇya-piṇḍa, un-stamped metallic currency mentioned in the Rig-Veda, 69, 70, 168, 178, 194-95.
Hūṇa, 18.
Huvishka, the Kushana king, 18, 23; inscriptions of, 4; coins of, 15, 17-8, 22.

I

Indian ocean, silver fish hooks current as money in, 136-37.
Indo-Bactrian Greek princes, the, 2, 4, 33, 35-6; coins of, 24, 32, 34.
Indo-Bactrian Greeks, 149-50, 199, 206.
Indo-Grecian kings, use of nickel in the coinage of, 143-44.
Indo-Parthian coins, 199.
Indo-Parthian kings, the, 2,
Indo-Sassanian coins, 207.
Indo-Scythian kings, the, 2, 8; coins of 7, 19, 35, 199.
Indo-Scythians, the, 3.
Indra, his image offered as a fetish for ten cows, mentioned in the Rigveda, 171.
Iran, 206.
Irānian divinities on Kushana coins, 15.

J

Janaka, King of Videha, 58-60.
Janapada, democracy confined to a province, 5-7, 13, 152, 193, 196.
Jānapada, the people of a province, 6, 13.
Janapade lup, a Sūtra in Pāṇini, 11.
Jātakas, the, 46-9, 52-4, 61-2, 77-9, 81, 87, 112, 142, 179-82, 185-86, 192, 194.
Jayadāman, a Kshatrapa ruler, 19.
Jeta, Prince, 149.
Jñānadeva, the earliest poet-saint of Mahārāshṭra, 147.
Johiyas (Johiya-bar), 11-12.
Justin, 2, 26.

K

Kadambas, lead coins issued by, 143.
Kāḍasa, legend on some very ancient coins (cast), 149.
K.dphises I, a Kushana king, 200.
Kāhan, the modern form of Sanskrit Kārshāpaṇa, 188.
Kākaṇī (Kākaṇika), 112, 156, 185.
Kākaṇikā, a small token coin, 77, 79.
Kākiṇī (Kākaṇikā), 87, 185.
Kākshīvat, a Vedicpoet-priest, 64.
Kalachuris, gold coins of, 209.
Kalhaṇa, 126.
Kalpasūtra, a Jaina canonical work, 67.
Kāmasūtra, 176.
Kāmbojas, the, 25.
Kāñchana-Drammas, 209.
Kaṇherī cave inscription, 209.
Kanishka, the Kushana king, 4, 16, 72, 73; coins of, 15-6, 203.
Kapardaka, a cowrie, 139, 176-77.
Kapardaka Purāṇa, mentioned in the Sena copper-plates, 139, 176.
Kāpiśi, 34.
Karamḍāṇḍā, inscribed Liṅga in the village of, 21.
Karsha, the name of a weight standard, 82-3, 86-7, 89-94, 111, 184-85, 189; a coin, 187.
Kārshāpaṇas, a class of coins, 39, 40, 42-5, 50, 54, 62, 75, 77-96, 100, 102-03, 105-09, 111-16, 118, 120-21, 126, 130-31, 133, 140, 147, 148, 157, 161-63, 167, 179, 180, 184-98, 200, 205, 207, 210-11.
Kārshāpaṇī, Kārshāpaṇa mentioned thus in Govindapāla's Gayā stone inscription, 188.
Kārttikeya, a Hindu deity, 22-3.
Karwar district, lead coins found in, 143.
Kashmir, coins of the Kidara-Kushanas found in, 205.
Kāśi, 50, 52.
Kāśikā, 83, 132-33, 205.
Kassite cylinders, 107.
Kaṭhaka-Saṁhitā, its mention of *hiraṇya-Kṛishṇala*, 60.
Kathāsaritsāgara, 131.
Kātyāyana, 55, 82, 130, 132.
Kātyāyana Smṛiti, 184-86, 188-89, 204, 210-11.
Kaurama, the king of the Rushamas, 64.
Kauṭilya, 5, 87, 89, 90, 92-4, 112, 125-26, 129-30, 156-63, 180.

Kaviśiye Nagaradevatā, Kharoshṭhī legend on the reverse of some coins of Eucratides, 33.
Kedāra, a coin denomination mentioned in the *Kāśikāvṛitti* 133, 205.
Kennedy, James, 39, 42-4, 71.
Khāravela, the ruler of Kaliṅga, 127.
Kidāra, the name occurring on the obverse of all the coins of the Kidāra-Kushanas, 205.
Kidāra-Kushanas, coins of the, 205.
Kistvaens, 96, 108.
Ki-to-lo, the leader of the great Yuch-ti as known from Chinese sources, 295.
Knossos, 106.
Kolhapur province, potin coinage in, 143, 145.
Kophen, the, 32.
Kṛishṇa, 35.
Kṛishṇala, a class of coins, 60-3, 70, 179;
—— weight standard, 86, 89, 92-3, 173-74, 180.
Kshaudrakas, the, use of nickel known to this Indian tribe, 144.
Kshīrasvāmin, the Commentator of Amara, 82, 133.
Kuhaka-Jātaka, 48.
Kujula Kadphises, 4.
Kumāra, a Hindu deity, 22-3;
—— figured on the coins of Huvishka, 18, 22.
Kumāradevī, wife of Chandragupta I, 9-10.
Kuru-Pañchāla country, 58.
Kuśaṇa, a coin denomination, 199, 200.
Kushana coinage, 22, 85, 203-04.
Kushanas, the, 2, 3, 15, 16, 18, 19, 181, 190, 199, 201-04.
Kuṭumbika, 48.

L

Lakshaṇādhyaksha, 128, 156-57.
Lakshmaṇa-Sena, 139.
Lekha, the art of writing, 124-25, 127-28.
Lekhaka, 125.
Lichchhavayaḥ, legend on the reverse of some of Chandragupta I's coins, 9.
Lichchhavidauhitra, a title adopted by Samudragupta, 9.
Lichchhavis, the, 9-10.
Līlāvatī, 190.

Liṅga, Siva worshipped in this form, 19-21.
Lydians, the, 110.
Lysias, silver coins of, 40.

M

Macedonians, the, 152.
Madhyamikā, a city identified with Nagari, 13 14.
Mādhyamikā country, 7, 13.
Mahābhārata, 5, 11, 13, 170.
Mahābhāshya of Patañjali, 14, 20, 22, 57.
Mahākshatrapa Rudrasena III, lead coins of, 143.
Mahākshatrapas, potin coins issued by, 145.
Mahārāshṭra, 67, 146-47, 191.
Mahārathīs, lead coins issued by, 143.
Mahāsena, a Hindu deity, 22-3;
—— figured on the coins of Huvishka, 18, 22.
Mahāsudassana Sutta, 102.
Mahāvagga, the, 124, 128.
Mahāvīra, 67.
Mālava, the name of a *gaṇa*, 193.
Mālavas, the, 5, 12-3, 144.
Malcolm, Sir John, 153.
Malli, the, 144.
Malloi, the, 12.
Mālwa, 18, 143, 145.
Manusaṁhitā, 60, 81-3, 86, 89, 92-3, 111, 179-86, 188-91. 199
Marmora, sea of, 136.
Marshall, Sir John, 40.
Māsha, a unit in the weight standard, 52-3, 89, 90, 111-12, 115-18, 120-21, 161, 174, 185-86, 188-90, 210.
Māshaka, a coin of one *māsha* in weight, 53, 62, 78-9, 87, 92-3, 111, 131, 140-41, 145, 156.
Māshaka-rūpa (Māshaka), a token coin, 131.
Mathurā, 35, 193, 136.
Mauryas, the, 57, 88.
Max Müller, Prof, 72-3.
Medinī, 170.
Mediterranean sea, 137.
Megasthenes, 35.
Menander, silver coins of, 40.

Mihirakula, coins of, 18.
Minoan Style, 106.
Mirat-i-Ahmadi, 117.
miskal, 73-4.
Mount Meru, 105-6.

N

Nagaradevatā, the city deity, 34.
Nagarī, the findspot of the Sibi coins, 13.
Nāgojibhaṭṭa, 57.
Nahapāna, 199, 200.
Naigama, democracy confined to a town, 5, 6;
—— coins issued by, 152.
Naihati grant of Ballāla Sena, 139.
Naishkika, a mint master, 133.
Nāṇaka, a coin denomination, 161.
Nandipada, a symbol, 197.
Nārada, his reference to Kārshāpaṇas, 82, 187.
Nāsik cave inscription, 183, 191, 199.
Negamā (*Naigamāḥ*) a word engraved on the obverse of a type of coins found in the Punjab, 6, 154, 197.
Nepāl, 9, 170.
Nidānakathā, mention of lead Kārshāpaṇas in, 142.
Nishka, mentioned as necklace in the vedas, 65-6, 68-9.
Nishkas, a class of gold coins, 45, 48-50, 53, 55-6, 61-3, 64-6, 68-70, 72-4 76-7, 83, 168, 178-79, 181-83, 209.
Nysa, 32.

O

Olbania, coins of, 137-38.
Olbia, currency of the city of, 136-37.
Orthagnes, a successor of Gondophares, 3.
Owls, the name of a class of coins current in Athens, 27-9.
Oxydracae, the, 144.

P

Pāda, a kind of coin, 59, 60, 111-12, 178-79, 186, 209-10.
Pāda-Kārshāpaṇa, 77, 87.

Paḍika, a coin mentioned in West India Cave inscriptions, 200.
Padyur, Roman coins found in, 202.
[*Pa*]*Khalavadi devadu*, Kharoshṭhī legend on the obverse of some coins, 34.
Pakores, 3.
Pala, the name of a weight standard, 86.
Pallas, the Greek goddess, 35.
Paṇa, 82, 88, 93, 112, 156, 158, 185, 188-90, 210.
Pañchāla, 193, 196.
Panchanan Mitra, 107, 135.
Pañchāyat, 208.
Pañchiyaka-dramma, 208.
Pāṇḍukuris (Pāṇḍukulis), Primitive tombs in South India, 108-10, 167.
Pāṇḍus, 109.
Pāṇini, 11, 20, 24-5, 29, 34, 45-7, 55, 60, 70, 83, 130, 132, 134, 169-71, 179.
Pantaleon, 35, 143.
Pārīkshika, 158.
Pāṭaliputra, 9, 10, 99, 100.
Patañjali, 14, 20, 22, 130, 132.
Pātimokkha, 134.
Paura, the townspeople, 6.
Pāvlā (or Pavli), a Marāṭhī term meaning one-fourth of the standard coin, 60.
Pearse, Col. 145.
Percy Gardner, 35-6.
Philoxenus, coins of, 35,40.
Phocæa, coinage of, 6.
Phrygian cap, 36.
Pliny, 202.
Pratihāra dynasty, 206, 208.
Prinsep, James, 38,40,42.
Ptolemy, 4.
Pudukottah State, temple coins struck in, 153.
Punch-marked coins, 39-41,88.
Purāṇa, Punch-marked coins known as, 82,84,92,94, 96, 114-16, 120, 139, 176, 180, 192.
Pushkalāvatī, 34.
Pushpapura, 9.
Puṭalya, a Marāṭhī term denoting gold coins as well as necklaces made of them, 67.

Q

Quintus Curtius, 144.

R

Rājagriha, 124, 186.
Rājanya, a Janapada, 7, 193.
Rājasūya, 150.
Rājataraṅginī, 126, 131, 204.
Rājputana, 169, 189, 208, 211.
Rāmachandra, the Yādava King, 147.
Rāmāśramī, a commentator of Amara, 82.
Rāmāyaṇa, 104.
Rañjubula, lead coins of, 143.
Rapson, Prof., 42, 45, 84, 111, 155-56, 202.
Rati, weight standard, 86, 90, 92, 111-13, 173-75, 180, 190.
Ratnas, Seven, 102.
Rhys Davids, Prof., 46, 59, 125-26, 145;
————Mrs., 111.
Ridgeway, Prof., 136, 169.
Ṛigveda, 64-6, 71, 73, 168, 171-72.
Rock Edict XIII of Aśoka, 25, 27.
Roman coins, 201-03.
Rudra, 66, 68.
Rudradāman, 11, 19.
Rudrasena III, Mahākshatrapa, 143.
Rūpa, signifying symbol or a figure on a coin, 68-9, 140-41, 145;
————denoting the science of coinage, 124-29;
————a class of coins, 131, 135, 138, 175-76.
Rūpadarśaka, examiner of coins (Kauṭilya), 126-30, 157, 159-60.
Rūpaka, coined money, 131, 187.
Rūpasūtra, the science of coinage, 129, 132, 165-66.
Rūpasutta, 126, 128.
Rūpatarka, examiner of coins (Patañjali), 130.
Rūpika, 157-58.
Rūpya, a coin denomination, 68, 132-35, 138, 175-76, 205.
Rūpyādhyaksha, a mint-master (Amara), 133, 156.
Rushamas, the, 64.

S

Sabaean, 28.
Śabdakalpadruma, 73.
Saint Thomas, legend of the Christian Apostle, 3.
Śākya Putra Śramaṇas, 124-25.
Sāmanta Pāsādikā, reference to Kārshāpaṇa in, 81.
Saṁgha, a form of government, 5, 6;
———Buddhist community, 131.
Saṁhitā Period, Śatamāna coins in the, 58.
Saṁhita portions of the Vedas, 70, 172-73, 178.
Śaṁkarārya, the commentator of Vātsyāyana's *Kāmasūtra*, 176-77.
Saṁkhapāla Jātaka, 52.
Samudragupta, 9, 11.
Sannidhātṛi, an officer in the Treasury (Kauṭilya), 159.
Śaśāṅka, King of Gauḍa, 18, 21.
Sassanian civilisation, 206-07.
Sassanian coinage, 208.
Śatamānas, a class of gold coins, 45, 55-8, 62-3, 70, 76, 150, 178-80, 182-83, 193
Śatapatha Brāhmaṇa, 56-8, 63, 150, 178, 193.
Śātavāhana, 185, 193.
Saubhūti, 31.
Sauvarṇika, 127-28, 160.
Sāyaṇa, 57.
Scandinavia, coins of Kanishka dug up in, 203.
Scytho-Sassanians, Śiva worshipped by, 17.
Seleucos, 26.
Semitic, 28.
Sena dynasty of Bengal, 176.
Sewell, Mr. Robert, 153.
Shaṭtriṁśat, 82, 84.
Shekel, 73, 119, 122.
Śibi, king of, 49.
Śibi Janapada, coins of, 7, 13, 14, 193.
Sigloi, Persian silver coins, 28, 119, 121.
Silāhāra dynasty, 208.
Sīsa-kāhāpana, lead Kārshāpaṇas mentioned in the *Nidāna-kathā*, 142.
Śiva, 15-22, 35.
Śiva-bull type, found on the coins of Śaśāṅka, 18.
Śiva-worship, at first not identical with Liṅga-worship, 19.

Siyadoṇī inscription, 208-09.
Skanda, a Hindu deity, 22-3;
———figured on the coins of Huvishka, 18, 22.
Smith, V. A., 39, 42-4, 71, 110, 119-20, 122, 141, 151, 154-55, 195, 202.
Smṛitis, 155, 179, 191.
Sophytes, 29, 30, 31, 33.
Southern Arabia Felix, 28.
Spalahores, brother of Vonones, 3.
Spalirises, the Indo Scythian Prince, 3, 4.
Spooner, D. B., 97, 114, 120, 155.
Śrī, the goddess of beauty, description of, 67.
Śrīmad Ādivarāha,—208.
Sriñjaya, 69.
Srī-Somaladevī, Queen of Ajayadeva, the Chauhan prince, 209.
Stein, Sir Aurel, 126, 131.
Strabo, 2, 26.
Strato, lead coins of, 143.
Stūpas, silver denarii of the Consular Period found in, 201.
Sungod, radiate figure of,—in the coins, 35.
Surāshṭra, 18.
Suśruta, 111.
Sūtras of Pāṇini, 45-7, 55, 60, 70, 130, 132, 169-70, 179.
Suvarṇa, a class of gold coins, 50-1, 57-8, 61-3, 70, 76-7, 89-92, 178-79, 183-84, 189, 191-92, 204, 209.
Suvarṇa-māsha, a standard of weight, 90.
Suvarṇa-Māshaka, a class of smaller gold coins, 52.
Suvarṇarūpakas, gold coins, 131.
Svaidāyana-Saunaka, 63-4.
Svastika, a symbol, 103-05.
Syrian Empire of Antiochus Theos, 26.

T

Taittiriya Brāhmaṇa, 58, 60, 178.
Taittiriya Saṁhitā, 58, 174, 178.
Takshaśilā, 99-100.
Talent type, 119.
Ṭaṅkapati, a mint-master, 133.
Tarpaṇdīghī Plates of Lakshmaṇasena, 139.
Tāratuṁśabhavana, 52,
Taxila, coins found at, 40.

Taxila mark, 98.
Telephus, coins of, 35.
Tetrobolus, 119, 121.
Theobald, 101, 103, 106-07, 164.
Thomas, Edward, 39, 42, 65, 71, 73-4, 95, 180.
Tiastenes of Ozene, Chashṭana mentioned thus by Ptolemy, 4.
Tickal, the smaller denomination of weight used in Burma, 62.
Ṭīkāsarvasva, 133.
Trasareṇu, the smallest mote observable in a sun beam—the smallest unit in the Indian metrical system, 174.
Travancore, old coinage of, 142.
Tri-Māshaka, 77, 87.
Triobolus, 119, 121.
Triśālā, the mother of Mahāvīra, 97.
Tushāspa, a Persian name adopted by a Greek in the time of Aśoka, 31.

U

Udayabhadra, 52-3.
Udayabhadrā, 52.
Udayagiri hill, 127.
Udaya Jātaka, 52.
Uddālaka Āruṇi, 63.
Ujjain Symbol, 107.
Ukshan, 17.
Umeśa, 17.
Upāli, 124-25, 127-28.
Upanishads, reference to coins in, 55.
Ushavadāta, son-in-law of Nahapāna, 13, 199, 200.

V

Vāchaspatya, references to Kārshāpaṇas in previous works quoted in, 73, 82.
Vajjian Bhikshus, 131.
Valarāma, the Hindu God, 35.
Vallabhiṭṭhā, 139.
Varāhamihira, 13.

Varahran V, coins of, 18
Vārāṇasī, 50.
Vāsudeva, the Hindu God, 33.
Vasudeva, the Kushana King, 18, 20;
—— inscriptions of 4;
—— coins of, 15, 17.
Vatasvaka, legend on some very ancient coins, 149, 196-97.
Vātsyāyana, 176.
Vedas, reference to coins in the, 54-5, 90.
—— the age of, 71, 78.
Vesali, 130.
Vessantara Jātaka, 49.
Vidiśā, 85, 88, 99, 100, 161, 185, 190.
Vigrahapāla, 208.
Vigrahapāliya-dramma, 208.
Viḷivāyakura, potin coins issued by, 143-44.
Viṁsopaka, coined money, 187, 189, 209-10.
Vinayapiṭaka, 87, 111, 140, 186.
Viśākha, a Hindu deity, 22-3;
—— figured on the coins of Huvishka, 18, 22.
Viss, the higher denomination of weight used in Burma, 62.
Viśuddhimāgga, 99, 100, 147, 159.
Vonones, the Indo-Scythian prince, 3.
Vṛishṇis, coins of the, 5.
Vyājī, 157.
Vyavahāra, 127.

W

Wales, coins of Kanishka dug up in, 204.
Walsh, Mr., 98-9, 165.
Weber, Prof., 42.
Wema Kadphises, 4, 15, 84.
Western Kshatrapas, the, 4, 8, 101.
West India Cave Inscriptions, 185, 187.
Wilson, H. H., 38, 42.
Wilson, Mr. Thomas, 104.
Winternitz, Prof., 71, 167.

Y

Yājñavalkya, 59, 85, 111, 161, 179-81, 184-85, 199.
Yaśaskara, a king, 131.
Yaudheyas, the, 5, 11, 193.
Yavanānī, the writing of the Greeks, 24, 29.
Yavanas, the, 24-7, 29, 31.
Yazdani, Mr., 106.
Yonas, the Greeks thus referred to in Aśoka inscriptions, 25-6.
Ysamotika, the father of Chashṭana, 18.

Z

Zeus, 33-5.